As Vice President and Director of Personnel for N W Ayer Incorporated, **Edward J. Rogers** has personally conducted thousands of job interviews. He holds a Masters in Counseling from Fordham University and is a graduate of Cornell University's School of Industrial and Labor Relations. He has spoken at college campuses across the nation and is the author of numerous articles on careers, employment, and related subjects.

Getting Hired

Everything You Need to Know
about Resumes, Interviews,
and Job-Hunting Strategies

EDWARD J. ROGERS

A SPECTRUM BOOK

Prentice-Hall, Inc., *Englewood Cliffs, New Jersey 07632*

Library of Congress Cataloging in Publication Data

Rogers, Edward J.
    Getting hired.

    (A Spectrum Book)
    Bibliography: p.
    Includes index.
    1.   Applications for positions.   2.   Resumes
(Employment)   3.   Employment interviewing.   4.   Job
hunting.   I. Title.
HF5382.7.R62   650.1'4   81-12100
                                           AACR2

ISBN 0-13-354605-5

ISBN 0-13-354597-0 {PBK.}

This Spectrum Book is available to businesses and organizations
at a special discount when ordered in large quantities. For
information, contact Prentice-Hall, Inc., General Book Marketing,
Special Sales Division, Englewood Cliffs, N.J. 07632.

10   9   8   7   6

Editorial/production supervision
and interior design by Kimberly Mazur
Cover illustration by Mike Aron
Manufacturing buyer: Cathie Lenard

Prentice-Hall International, Inc., *London*
Prentice-Hall of Australia Pty. Limited, *Sydney*
Prentice-Hall of Canada, Ltd., *Toronto*
Prentice-Hall of India Private Limited, *New Delhi*
Prentice-Hall of Japan, Inc., *Tokyo*
Prentice-Hall of Southeast Asia Pte. Ltd., *Singapore*
Whitehall Books Limited, *Wellington, New Zealand*

For the hundreds of thousands of college students facing a major competitive challenge: finding and securing an entry-level position that will move them a major step toward career satisfaction.

Contents

Preface

This book was written to help you find a job in business, government, or education. It is directed specifically to college graduates-to-be, recent grads, and job hunters looking for entry level positions after having been away from the workworld for a while. No other book has all the features you'll find in this one:

- Complete and thorough coverage of every aspect of the job-seeking process including sources, networking, strategies, resumes and other written communications, interviews, productive use of time between interviews, job offers, negotiations, and starting off on the right foot.
- A practical approach which recognizes the special needs and particular problems faced by job seekers, and specific techniques for the resolutions of those problems. It explains *why* certain approaches or actions are recommended so that you have a better understanding of the process involved.
- A self-rating scale which enables you to see how you compare with your job-seeking competition.

- A highly useful "Job Search Control Sheet" which can be easily duplicated and used to keep track of job prospects and contacts.
- Five appendixes packed with information to broaden job-seeker knowledge and save you many hours hunting sources which can help you prepare an effective resume, get ready for successful interviews, and make wise employment-related decisions.
- Quoted contributions from successful professionals in business, education, and government, each of whom share personal perspectives on various aspects of the job-seeking process.

This book will show you how to increase your economic value by associating yourself with employers who are committed to helping their newly-hired neophytes fulfill individual potential through training and management development programs.

You will find specific recommendations here on how to apply your college education to the needs of the business, education, or government communities in ways that will result in superior income as well as greater self-fulfillment.

You will learn all about job-hunting guidelines and techniques—those that are well known and trustworthy, as well as those overlooked by most job seekers except for the top five percent. You will have the advantage of being better prepared than most of your competition; and as a result, you will have a better chance of getting hired into a desirable position.

Acknowledgments

A resource book such as this isn't written without input from numerous people and organizations.

Special appreciation goes to a cadre of professionals who, because of their contributions, inspiration, or encouragement, helped bring this book into being. My sincere thanks to Eugene Fixler, Jill Ghari, Marion Hajdu, Al Hegyi, Rev. Thomas Hennessy, S. J., Dick Joel, Doug Johnson, Len Lanfranco, Bill Luedke, Charlie Mauldin, Neal O'Connor, Maxine Paetro, Susan Poole, Anne Rogers, Michael Rogers, Ricki Rogers, Steven Rogers, David Rowe, Herman Slotkin, editor Mary Kennan, the dozens of professionals quoted throughout the book, and the many career counseling and placement office personnel with whom I've had contact.

A unique feature of this book is the extensive use of resumes and resume attachments actually written by graduating seniors. They have demonstrated their grasp of effective resume writing. With gratefulness and respect I thank Bill Bergman, Karl Dentino, Tim Kane, Maria Mirto, Rhonda Petrovsky, Judith Quittner, Neal Roher,

Holly Rosenthal, Susan Shaffer, Lori Spano (neé Silverstein), Edna Stern, Miriam Suchoff, and Lezli White.

My thanks to these organizations and publications for their gracious cooperation: Association of MBA Executives, College Placement Council, *Journal of College Placement*, Labor Market Information Network, Metropolitan New York College Placement Officers' Association, Northwestern University, *Occupational Outlook Quarterly*, *Personnel Journal*, and Prentice-Hall. Thanks also to those whose written materials provided especially helpful background data: American Personnel and Guidance Association, American Society for Personnel Administration, Catalyst, *College Placement Annual*, *Journal of College Student Personnel*, National Vocational Guidance Association, *Vocational Guidance Quarterly*, *The New York Times*, 13-30 Corporation, U.S. Department of Labor (Bureau of Labor Statistics), and University Communications, Inc.

Large numbers of interviewed graduating seniors, recent college grads, many librarians on college campuses across the country, friends in the career advisement community, and professional colleagues, all contributed to the store of knowledge and advice transmitted on these pages. Although unnamed, they are by no means unappreciated.

1

Rating Yourself as a Job Seeker

Those who interview you have a mission. They want to find and hire the very best candidates they can for their organization. Of course, "best" is defined in many ways, often subjectively, depending on the interviewer's orientation. But regardless of who is doing the interviewing, and no matter what the nature of the organization, virtually all interviewers share the experience and the feeling that an important part of being "the best" is how the candidate conveys his or her abilities, knowledge, and personality.

> The skills that make a person employable are not so much the ones needed on the job as the ones needed to get the job, skills like the ability to find a job opening, complete an application, prepare a resume, and survive an interview.
>
> OCCUPATIONAL OUTLOOK QUARTERLY
> U.S. DEPARTMENT OF LABOR

You are reading this book because you recognize that with the help of beneficial information and some useful strategies and techniques, you can improve your preparation and presentation for the

1

competitive arena of job-seeking. That's an important step because you will improve your standing among other applicants vying for the same jobs by successfully honing and projecting your presentation in these four key areas:

Information Gathering
Resumes and Other Written Communications
Networking
Presentation Skills

Before turning to the details involved in effectively and successfully applying your own efforts to the job-seeking process, take a few minutes to test yourself on how you currently rate as a job seeker. Four scales have been devised to help you judge your standing in each of the key areas. Score yourself by checking off the appropriate box at the bottom of each scale (the unnumbered boxes are half-way points, so that if you're between "Satisfactory" and "Very Good," your score for that area is 3½). Be as objective as you possibly can. Honesty with yourself will help you identify those areas which need the most improvement. Add your four area scores together for a total score, which is interpreted immediately following the four scales.

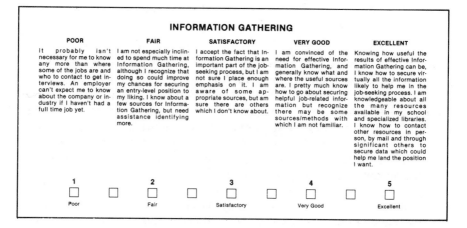

INFORMATION GATHERING

POOR	FAIR	SATISFACTORY	VERY GOOD	EXCELLENT
It probably isn't necessary for me to know any more than where some of the jobs are and who to contact to get interviews. An employer can't expect me to know about the company or industry if I haven't had a full time job yet.	I am not especially inclined to spend much time at Information Gathering, although I recognize that doing so could improve my chances for securing an entry-level position to my liking. I know about a few sources for Information Gathering, but need assistance identifying more.	I accept the fact that Information Gathering is an important part of the job-seeking process, but I am not sure I place enough emphasis on it. I am aware of some appropriate sources, but am sure there are others which I don't know about.	I am convinced of the need for effective Information Gathering, and generally know what and where the useful sources are. I pretty much know how to go about securing helpful job-related information but recognize there may be some sources/methods with which I am not familiar.	Knowing how useful the results of effective Information Gathering can be, I know how to secure virtually all the information likely to help me in the job-seeking process. I am knowledgeable about all the many resources available in my school and specialized libraries. I know how to contact other resources in person, by mail and through significant others to secure data which could help me land the position I want.
1 □	□ 2 □	□ 3 □	□ 4 □	□ 5 □
Poor	Fair	Satisfactory	Very Good	Excellent

RESUME AND WRITTEN COMMUNICATIONS

POOR	FAIR	SATISFACTORY	VERY GOOD	EXCELLENT
When I write my resume, it will probably reflect the fact that I have little or no idea of good resume content and structure. I doubt I could write an effective resume. My letter writing skills are admittedly poor; I have never written anything that was complimented for its style or content. I have a problem with proper sentence structure, grammar and logical organization of written presentations.	I think I know most of what belongs in a resume and how to put one together, but I am not very confident that the resume I write will be considered any better than ordinary by most employers. My writing skills are probably somewhat below average; rarely have I had positive feedback about my writing ability.	I am pretty sure I have a feeling for the content and form of a good resume, although the result of my efforts would probably not be what most employers would consider a better-than-good product. I can express myself reasonably well in writing, but I recognize that most of what I write would be termed "average" by most employers.	I am comfortable with my awareness of good resume content and form. I am reasonably confident that I can write a very good resume; however, I recognize that fine-tuning may result in an even more effective document. Generally, my writing skills are quite good although not unusual in their impact on others.	There is no doubt in my mind that I can write an outstanding resume; one to which a large majority of potential employers will respond positively. My other written communications are always effective; I am frequently praised by others for my ability with the written word.

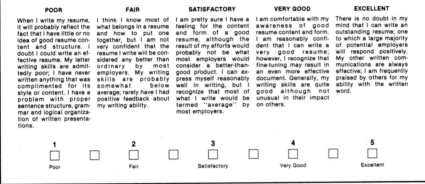

1   2   3   4   5

Poor   Fair   Satisfactory   Very Good   Excellent

NETWORKING

POOR	FAIR	SATISFACTORY	VERY GOOD	EXCELLENT
I am aware of only two or three ways of uncovering information about open jobs which might be of interest to me. I guess there are probably ways to increase the few choices I could have, but I do not know how to go about learning what they are.	I have an idea of what Networking is about, and could make a few contacts with potential employers as a result. But I realize that through greater effort I could substantially increase the quantity and quality of my contacts.	I know that through Networking I could develop several contacts and would have some options among potential employers of interest to me. However, I confess that developing additional job sources is probably necessary if I am to end up with a job which reasonably meets my entry-level goals.	I could do a good job of using Networking to my advantage. Through developed leads I could uncover a number of possible positions for myself, though I would like to be able to expand and/or sharpen my options even further.	I am sure I would be highly proficient at Networking. I could develop so many useful contacts that I would be aware of far more positions than I could hope to have time to investigate. I am certain that from among the options which would be available, there are several which would result in concrete offers closely matching my desires.

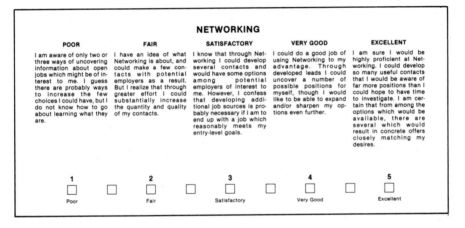

1   2   3   4   5

Poor   Fair   Satisfactory   Very Good   Excellent

PRESENTATION SKILLS

POOR	FAIR	SATISFACTORY	VERY GOOD	EXCELLENT
I must confess I would not make a good impression at interviews. My verbal skills are weak; I have trouble finding the "right" word, there are lots of ers and ahs in my speech. I do not project enthusiasm and other positive qualities when I talk. I do not know what "body language" is. I don't think what I wear to an interview matters much.	I would probably make only a fair impression at interviews. My verbal skills are on the weak side; I know there's a good deal of room for improvement. I need more information about how to dress for an interview and the importance of what I say with my "body language."	I think I would make an acceptable impression at interviews. I have average verbal skills; not especially memorable, but not damaging. I could improve some on the visual impact I have on others, both as to the way I dress and how I respond physically.	I believe I could make a quite good impression at interviews. My verbal skills are sound, though not exceptional. I am well aware of the importance of positive "body language" and proper attire, although I don't always measure up to my own awareness and standards.	I am sure I could make an outstanding impression when being interviewed. I have developed highly effective verbal skills. I am sure I would always impress an interviewer with my appearance and visual physical reactions.

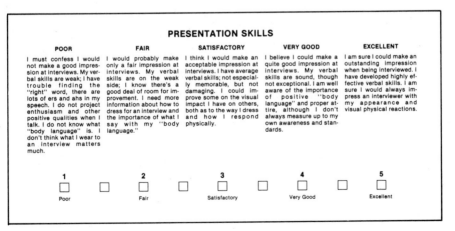

1   2   3   4   5

Poor   Fair   Satisfactory   Very Good   Excellent

EVALUATING YOUR SCORE
(SUM OF THE FOUR SCALES)

18 - 20   You are a rarity! You will most likely do extremely well in your job-seeking efforts. You have an unusually strong command of the techniques and strategies necessary to present yourself in the best light.

14 - 17½   You have reasonably good command of key elements in the job-seeking process. But competition is stiff; although you are more advanced than some of your contemporaries, you should make further efforts to improve your preparation.

10 - 13½   At this level, you are likely to have trouble impressing desirable potential employers. You will have to work hard at developing your job-seeking abilities and presentation if you are to avoid being overshadowed by the considerable number of those who score 14 or higher.

Fewer than 10   You have a long way to go before venturing out into the job market if you want to land a desirable position which will offer opportunity for personal development and career growth. Given the level of your skills at this time, you'll have to work very hard to bring about much needed improvement.

2

Locating
the Jobs

The first step in your job hunt must be to find out *where* the positions are which will come closest to meeting your goals.

> The process of job exploration begins with selecting four or five careers that are compatible with what you have learned about yourself. Look up these careers in the *Occupational Outlook Handbook* and the *Dictionary of Occupational Titles* to get a description of the career. Use directories and periodicals to get a "feel" for where these careers are used. Don't overlook the yellow pages, newspaper ads and other paper resources. Do some informational interviewing to gain further insight into requirements of these career fields.
>
> ADRIAN J. SEWALL, DIRECTOR
> OFFICE OF CAREER PLANNING AND PLACEMENT
> UNIVERSITY OF MAINE

Job opportunities are so closely tied to economic, social, and business trends that it would be ludicrous to attempt any sort of permanent analysis of the job market. No one can predict with certainty what future labor market conditions will be. In every occupation, a rise or fall in the demand for a product or service can (sometimes quickly) change both the number and nature of job openings. New inventions and technologies come along to create new jobs and eliminate old ones. Changes in the population makeup, retirement policies, and work attitudes all interact to create shortages in some areas, surpluses in others.

There are, however, guidelines for making your own analysis at the time your job hunt begins. It is important, first, to recognize a few basic facts about the job market which are relatively unaffected by changing trends. It is true that you may encounter difficulty in finding work if your chosen field is so small that few new openings occur each year or if it is so popular that it attracts many more applicants than there are jobs (journalism and education, for example, are now overcrowded). Yet even small or crowded occupations do provide some jobs, as do those which are experiencing slow growth or even declining. In such cases, you must be prepared to put greater effort, possibly a larger financial investment, and certainly more time into your search for work. Every occupation must replace workers who leave it. The Bureau of Labor Statistics' Occupational Outlook Handbook estimates that nearly two-thirds of all job openings are accounted for by replacements.

In most cases, your search in a field with few entry-level openings will be harder if you merely stick to the obvious approach of trying to land one of the relatively few traditional starting positions. Consider this option: if you can identify an emerging need in a career field which interests you, you have a strong selling point to employers who might otherwise not consider you. By looking ahead to newly-developing needs you may be able to approach employers with abilities, skills, and interests which enhance your chances of being considered a valuable addition to present staff. Think of fields such as bioengineering, time management, oceanography, word processing, solar energy, medical anthropology, consumer affairs, nuclear pharmacy, governmental regulation compliance, nautical archeology, technical writing, gerontology, and product safety, to mention just a few.

Just because your job market analysis may turn up discouraging statistics, do not let that necessarily deter you from a goal you know is right for you. Instead, be prepared for stiff competition and consider seriously any alternative approaches that can provide an entry into your first-choice job field.

A college graduate seeking a job should do homework on the company he/she is interested in . . . learn about its products or services; review recent articles from trade or newspapers; visit its facilities if they are open to the public.

RICHARD C. MARCUS, CHAIRMAN
NEIMAN-MARCUS

WHERE TO START

If your college has a placement office, there is no better place to find out what's going on in the fields which interest you. Placement offices are virtual storehouses of information and also serve as major links between students and employers. Their services are available even if you aren't a full-time or resident student, or a U.S. citizen. If you have ever taken even one course at a school, you're entitled to the help they can provide. If you've attended several colleges, you can use the facilities of each of them.

Long before graduation, it will pay to become a familiar face at your school's placement office. Its roster of summer jobs or internships can be invaluable in giving you exposure to careers you are considering. Three such summer, career-related jobs add up to almost a full year of work experience, which is a real plus on your resume. For contacts to acquire information about such positions, see Appendix A.

WHAT YOU CAN DO
ON YOUR OWN

Regardless of whether your school has a placement office, it's up to you to ferret out job market data on your own. Your school or public library should become a second home as you locate and study all you can about your chosen field(s) of interest.

Directories, bibliographies, self-help books, and informational and trade publications are your textbooks in this self-study job-market course. From them, you will become familiar with companies who are leading employers, their size and organizational structures, management personnel, geographic concentrations, and current trends. That means hours may be spent wading through stacks of printed matter. But when you're finished, you will have gained more than a speaking acquaintance of the work world in which you wish to function. "If you want a company to be interested in learning more about you, the best way to do it, in my opinion, is for you to take a prior interest in learning more about the company and the specific position before you apply," says Kenneth B. Hoyt, director of Career Education, U.S. Department of Education. Many a graduate-to-be has benefited from scrutinizing the reference section of a library. Only library science majors fail to register surprise at the large number of previously unknown resources packed with useful information for career explorers and job seekers.

To help you identify the "career bibles" which can be so useful for this phase of your job hunt, see the annotated resources in Appendix B. They will enable you to spot quickly the entries related to your information-gathering efforts. Spend time studying and using this appendix. It's a valuable shortcut which will save you many hours of research.

Trade publications (those aimed at a specific occupation) are required reading. If you don't know the names of professional periodicals in your chosen field, ask your librarian, then read several back issues as well as current ones. Aside from giving you valuable background information on possible job sources, this kind of research provides talking points (in the professional lingo) during future interviews, which is bound to be impressive to employers.

Industrial and craft unions are another valuable source of information. Learn about them. Visit local offices or write the nearest office for current literature. Some print bulletins, newsletters, and brochures that will fill you in on what's going on in that particular field, as well as their own activities.

The *Encyclopedia of Associations* will inform you about professional associations to contact for details on jobs, training, and scholarships available. Many libraries have copies of this valuable publication.

State and city employment services have up-to-the-minute listings on all openings in their areas, charge no fees, and sometimes have valuable studies on business trends. You'll find addresses and telephone numbers listed in local telephone directories; if you're researching from a distance, your library can help you locate them.

The Wall Street Journal has pages and pages of help-wanted ads, as do the vast majority of large-city daily newspapers. Study them for several weeks to get a picture of where openings are occurring. Even though many are for positions above the entry-level, you'll be able to spot growth trends, and growth means openings at the bottom as well as the top. If you do apply for a position advertised, be sure to save the ad for later reference.

A helpful and interesting resource for keeping up to date on workworld developments is the weekly "Careers" column in *The New York Times* (many libraries across the country have *The Times* — either the paper or on microfilm). A sampling of topics: "New Hope for Science and Arts," "Engineers: The Future Challenge," "Women's Expanding Sales Role," "Helping to Select a Field," "Retailers Offering Openings," "Agriculture: More than Farming," "New Field: Problems of Aging."

Modern technology is reflected in the Placement Reference Network (PREF) videodisc information service, installed at a number of college campuses, usually in placement and career information offices. Career choice and employment information is recorded by participating employers, permitting students to view various options on color TV monitors hooked up to PREF playback machines. Training program opportunities are described and company/industry data is presented much as a documentary film would be on a TV program. If your school participates, be sure to make use of this stimulating, fact-filled medium for learning more about potential employers.

The U.S. Office of Personnel Management (formerly the Civil Service Commission) publicizes job opportunities for civilian jobs with the government. Don't overlook this source; there is a wide variety of professional and technical positions to be filled based on examinations, education, and experience. You can get announcements of open jobs, brochures, and application forms by writing to: Office of Personnel Management, Washington D.C. 20415.

Bulletin boards in libraries, city or town halls, and courthouses often have local, state, or federal government-related positions posted.

If you find a geographic concentration of jobs in your field, write to local Chambers of Commerce for job-hunting leads. Find out about specialized state directories (for example, *Delaware Directory of Commerce and Industry, Georgia Manufacturing Directory, Directory of Utah Manufacturers*, and so on), writing to the appropriate state Chamber of Commerce, in the state's capital city, if copies are not available in your library.

KEEPING CURRENT

The sources mentioned above, in conjunction with Appendix B, are by no means the only ones available. There is a vast array of material, and new things are coming along all the time. So *be aware*, keep your eyes open, and stay in close touch with your librarian and placement office. Becoming a "research freak" at this stage of the job-seeking process can pay valuable dividends. Heed the advice of R. Manning Brown, Jr., chairman of the board, New York Life Insurance Company: "Learn as much as you can about the kinds of organizations within which you can achieve your goal. Your research will help you to understand what a company does, why it does it, and how it operates; you will then be able to speak intelligently about it when and if you are interviewed for a position."

IN BRIEF

In analyzing the job market you are about to enter, there are several important methods of gathering information: through your college placement office; through professional directories; through trade journals; through craft and professional unions; through professional associations; through business-oriented newspapers; and through myriad library sources. Such information, besides being useful in its own right, provides background for your next important step — making personal contacts, or *networking*.

3

People Who Can
Help You
Find Jobs

With the ability to secure background information on occupations and potential employers likely to be of interest to you, you can move on to an equally (if not more) productive phase of your market research: *personal contacts*. Awareness of a field's special language will serve you well now. Not only will your own conversation be impressive to those you approach, but what they have to say will have more meaning for you.

NETWORKING

The term *networking* is a popularly used buzzword for establishing connections in the work world. Connections can dramatically increase your understanding of various occupations, while at the same time broaden opportunities for you to locate a desirable position.

To find those contacts, start with your own family and friends of the family. Almost certainly you'll find leads. Even if no one you know is engaged in your choice of occupation, it's likely you'll discover friends of friends who are. Most will be happy to discuss the job situation with you. Even casual acquaintances will sometimes turn out to possess the very bit of information you need to direct your efforts most effectively.

Another, often overlooked, source of industry, government, and education contacts is your college faculty. Professors try to keep abreast of developments in their area of interest, and many have influential contacts actively engaged in some phase of work associated with it. Also, drop by the alumni office on campus and inquire about graduates who have entered the career you've chosen. That "old school tie" is one of the strongest contacts, giving you a ready-made basis for asking about industry-wide opportunities.

Don't forget college classmates, fellow employees at part-time or summer jobs, sports partners, or any others with whom you have contact. You do not have to know someone well for him or her to be a valuable resource. Networking can be successfully accomplished through tangential as well as close relationships.

The importance of personal contacts cannot be over-emphasized. They provide a springboard to actual job interviews when you plan your overall strategy for finding a job. Remember, it's human nature to enjoy giving advice, and most people already established in their field will give willingly of their time to anyone considering it. Many a busy executive will gladly respond to a short note asking for an interview to discuss your future, even if you have no other introduction.

> Use every personal contact you have to send out the message that you want a job and, if you have something specific in mind, what it is.
>
> DR. CAROL FINN MEYER, VICE PRESIDENT
> CROSSLEY SURVEYS

"Don't be shy. Ask every family friend, use every connection to help you," says Whit Hobbs, creative consultant to *The New Yorker Magazine* and Sperry Corporation, and monthly columnist in *ADWEEK*. "Ask every person you see for an interview if he or she will send you to one additional person. With every interview, you learn something, you get better at it, and you improve the odds."

What these people can tell you is what it is like from the inside which, after all, is what you need to know. Personal information outweighs most of what you can read on the subject, as well as anything personnel people who are looking for recruits can tell you. It's the functional specialists, those doing what you hope someday to do, who can tell you what it's really like and where openings are most likely to be found.

Perhaps even more important, every contact is a potential lead to *other* contacts. You will be plugging into the network of the work world, and when the time comes to approach the job market, those contacts will be worth their weight in gold. The phrase frequently applied to this activity is "interviewing for information." It often leads to concrete job opportunities; it is a two-edged sword that can work very well for you.

SOURCES

How do you find the people whom you would like to interview for information?

- Your school's placement office may have a list of volunteers, ready to meet with you.
- Ask family, professors, clergy, and friends for names of people whom they know are working in the type of position about which you would like to know more.
- Contact community-service groups (for example, Rotary Club, Toastmasters, Lions Club, Chamber of Commerce) and inquire about who you could meet with.
- Professional associations (some of which have on-campus chapters) and unions can be excellent sources.
- Local employers (Take the direct-contact route. The Yellow Pages can be especially helpful for contacts).
- The editors of trade or professional publications have a wide array of contacts in their respective fields.

Once you've made a contact, you want to be sure you make maximum use of the time the person is willing to spend with you. Read up on the career in which the person you'll be interviewing is engaged. At the very least, look up the position in the U.S. government's *Occupational Outlook Handbook* and the *Dictionary of Occupational Titles*. Check your placement office and the careers section of your library for additional information.

It is imperative for today's youthful job-seekers to know what job or related job they want, and become acquainted with the market place in that field. This can be accomplished by making placement office contacts (and) interviewing with potential employers.

DR. JAMES PEAL, MANAGER
COLLEGE RELATIONS PROGRAM
U.S. OFFICE OF PERSONNEL MANAGEMENT

SECURING INFORMATION

Armed with some knowledge about your interviewee's occupation, and having your own interests, abilities, and values in mind, you will be far better prepared to capitalize on your interview for information. Here is a list of questions which will help you get the information you want:

- Please give me a general description of the work you do.
- What is your typical work day like?
- What are the things you find most rewarding about your work?
- What are the toughest problems you encounter in your job?
- What are the frustrations in your work? What compromises are most difficult to make?
- If you could change your job in some way, what would that change be?
- Does your job affect your personal life? If so, how?
- What educational degrees, licenses, or other credentials are required for entry and advancement in your kind of work? Are there any which are preferred or helpful, although not required?
- What are the trade/professional groups to which you belong, and which you find most beneficial in your work? Do any of them assist college seniors interested in entry-level positions in your field?
- What abilities, interests, values, and personality characteristics are important for effectiveness and satisfaction in your field?
- How do people usually learn about job openings in your field?
- What types of employers, other than your own, hire people to perform the kind of work you do? Do you know of any which offer entry-level training programs or opportunities?
- If you were hiring someone today, for an entry-level position in your field, what would be the most critical factors influencing your choice of one candidate over another?
- What are typical earnings at various stages of a career in your field?
- Is there anything else you think I would benefit from knowing about the field you're in?

These questions provide the framework for a meaningful information interview. Although you may not have the chance to ask all of them, copy them onto a single sheet of paper and take them along with you. You'll help yourself and the person you're interviewing by being well-prepared for your meeting. You will also make a better impression on your interviewee. Remember that an interview for information may lead to the establishment of a relationship which could result in a permanent, part-time, or summer job offer to you, either from the person you're interviewing, or someone that person refers you to after meeting with you.

Within two or three days of the meeting, send a thank-you note. It will show you're courteous and remind the recipient about your session.

In the Fall 1980 issue of *Journal of College Placement*, Joann Javonovich and Sharyn L. Tanguay, from the Career Development Center at the University of Southern California, cited these advantages of networking:

"1. Increases skills and self-confidence in obtaining information from a large number of resources.
  2. Fosters an attitude of being in control of seeking, obtaining, and using information to make informed judgments and decisions.
  3. Provides a new perspective and understanding on the usefulness of contacts.
  4. Builds a referral base for continued career exploration or actual job search."

The time and effort involved in arranging and conducting information interviews will be well worth your while. C. Peter McColough, chairman of the Xerox Corporation, advises: "When (students become) aware of the jobs that utilize their knowledge and university training, and gain an understanding of what job holders actually do, they are much better prepared to choose industries, companies, and jobs that fit their interests, abilities, and lifestyles."

IN BRIEF

Networking is an extremely helpful method of gathering information and possibly locating an employer. In conjunction with the resources described in Chapter 2, networking rounds out your basic knowledge of the job market. You are now ready to plot effective job-hunting strategy to help land you in the ranks of those employed in positions providing psychological as well as monetary rewards.

Successful Job-Finding Strategies

Now that you have an overview of the job market and just where the jobs you want are located, it's time to get down to the basics of plotting a strategy that will bring in as many desirable job offers as possible.

As this book is written, the job outlook in the United States varies almost from day to day, and certainly from authority to authority, chiefly because of uncertain economic trends. The effects of further inflation and the part government policies will play are largely unpredictable. But regardless of what the job market is, you have by this time become your own marketing expert. You know the situation and you know where the opportunities — limited or plentiful — lie. Although things look a little bleak at the moment, this is not the time for discouragement. It means only that you must plan your offensive even more carefully, be better informed and better prepared than your competitors. Moreover, you must be ready to make the job of finding a job an all-out effort. If there are fewer jobs available, you must try all the harder, and see many more potential employers.

Knowing how to apply for a job is as important in getting hired as knowing how to do the job, or being able to learn it.

EMPLOYERS' VIEWS ON HIRING AND TRAINING
NEW YORK STATE DEPARTMENT OF LABOR

It would be nice if we could set down a simple formula that would guarantee results. The truth is, however, that there is no one best way to launch a job search. In fact, successful job seekers (those who find highly desirable positions) frequently mount a multi-faceted campaign, employing several approaches concurrently. The job-seeker who says: "I'll try this and see whether it works. If not, I'll try that next," loses precious time, is less competitive, and denies him/herself the opportunity to bring together several job offers at about the same time. Having the chance to *choose* from among several offers is an ideal circumstance which deserves the extra energy required.

You may find your first job through a newspaper ad, a college placement office, a letter you write, a friend, an employment agency, or as a walk-in applicant. You may try a maverick approach and, if it's appropriate, it may land you the job you want. All these will be discussed later in this chapter.

Bear in mind this extremely important advice for job-seekers: no matter what kind of campaign you undertake, to be successful *it must reflect you favorably.* Demonstrating your positive assets can be even more important than your job-hunting methods. Every step you plan must feel comfortable and natural to you, and help you look good. If, over time, you still find yourself without a job, look again at your self-evaluation as revealed by your resume or interview conduct; then get advice from others who can help you modify your presentation and techniques. Always make such alterations within the context of your own personality and your own style, but don't be bashful about presenting yourself in the best light possible.

Focus on the answer to the following rhetorical question: "Why should they want to hire me, rather than one of the other seventy-three applicants?" Certainly, phoniness or pretense will work against you in your efforts to shine. However, there is nothing wrong with emphasizing your strengths, uniqueness, demonstrated abilities, energy, and motivation when presenting yourself in writing, in person, or on the phone.

It is true that if you are skilled in the techniques of selling, you may be able to sell yourself as something you are not, and land a job that looks better than most. It is also true that if you follow such a course, you will find it difficult, if not impossible, to follow through on the job. Resignation or dismissal will be only a matter of time. Recognize right now — at the start of your search — that certain types of people belong in certain jobs. You should strive to make it as easy as possible for those who are hiring to see clearly where your unique skills and abilities and personality fit into the scheme of things.

Now, on to that strategy!

SIX BASIC STEPS

While there is no magic formula, there are very definite steps to the job you want, no matter which path you use to reach it. They can seldom be bypassed, and they follow in logical sequence. You must:

1. Pinpoint the potential employers to be approached.
2. Decide on the best means of approach.
3. Present your resume in the most effective way you can.
4. Be interviewed by employer representatives and be well-perceived.
5. Negotiate acceptable job terms.
6. Be prepared to get off to a favorable start when you report for work.

These are the six essential steps — a master pattern from which to tailor your personal marketing program. Each part of the process will have your individual stamp on it. Your job now is to plan each one so carefully and so selectively that there will be little or no lost time and motion between the first day of your search and your first day on the job.

WHICH ORGANIZATIONS TO APPROACH

Because of your research to find out where the jobs are, you already have a list of corporations, government agencies, educational institutions, consulting firms, or other possible employers which meet the job and personal requirements you've set for yourself. Now it is time to look at each one very closely to determine which should go at the top of your list. Your role at this point is that of investigator. You must find out everything you can about every potential employer, and your examination must be from the viewpoint of a future employee.

You will, first of all, want to know each employer's history and its prospects for future growth. Is it well established, with a record of stability? Or newly formed, with exciting — even if unproven and somewhat risky — plans for the future? Have top executives risen from within the organization, or is top talent imported? These are important considerations which could have a profound effect on your own future, and it is surprisingly easy to get this kind of information.

A short, polite note to the public relations or corporate communications department of any organization will usually result in useful written materials: an annual report*; a short organizational history, if it is available; product information; publicity pieces and article reprints; and a variety of other helpful facts. Even if you are going into a non-profit area such as education or government service, an annual report, which most organizations have in one form or another, reveals much about sound management — a matter of vital concern to anyone considering employment.

This kind of public-oriented information can be very helpful by providing the background you need to do the homework necessary for effective and impressive written and oral communications. The insights you can gain make you a knowledgeable applicant, the kind of person to which potential employers respond positively.

If you know someone employed in one of your target organizations, so much the better. Inside information is invaluable and can help you determine to some extent the chemistry of the organization. Even if you don't know an employee, ask around to find out if someone you know knows someone. Check to see if your alumni office keeps or publishes a directory showing business affiliations; then contact any alumni now working with target companies. Almost everyone is willing and eager to talk about where they work. Your job is to find people who work for your targets, then *listen*!

Don't overlook the facilities right at your doorstep: those in your school. It has a vested interest in turning out graduates who are successful. Placement directors, administrators, and professors are important sources of information about organizations which can use your education.

For an inside look at target organizations, even when you have no employee contact, simply call or write the personnel department of each. Ask them to send descriptions of employee benefits, training and management development programs, pre-supervisory and executive training opportunities, and promotion policies. Many organizations have on hand a packet of just such information used in recruit-

---

*For a free copy of "What Else Can Financial Statements Tell You?", write to American Institute of Certified Public Accountants, 1211 Avenue of the Americas, New York, N.Y. 10036.

ing new employees. But don't stop your investigation there. As detailed in Chapter 2, pay a visit to your local public or school library. There is a wealth of valuable information on the library shelves, yours for the asking. The librarian can often point out specialized references little known outside a particular field. And there are a number of well-known directories which provide important background intelligence on potential employers. They contain corporate histories, sales, products and services, key names and titles (so important for you to know), and contact information. For an annotated bibliography of such sources, see Appendix B.

These are specific avenues of investigation. Just as important is a continuing awareness of what is going on in your career field(s) of interest. Promotions and transfers reported in newspapers say something about the organization involved. *The Wall Street Journal, Business Week, Forbes,* and pertinent sections of other leading publications, as well as trade and professional sources and your local newspapers, will keep you abreast of developments and perhaps suggest other sources of information about your target organizations. Train yourself to read or listen to newscasts with the view of gleaning as much hard information and "feel" about organizations reported on, as you can. Be a sponge: soak up every little bit of data on the potential employers you'll be approaching.

PLANNING YOUR APPROACH

To keep things orderly, it's suggested that you transform your list of target employers into a file of *Job Search Control Sheets,* similar to Figure 4.1. Make a separate sheet for each organization, filing them in alphabetical order. Not only will these sheets help you organize your efforts in the most effective, time-saving manner, they will, as things progress, give you a quick checklist of what remains to be done or the outcome of actions you have already taken.

Using Figure 4.2 as a model, let's look at what your Job Search Control Sheet should show. Start by listing possible contacts, both within and outside the organization. The "Target Position(s)" column will include openings you've learned of from placement centers, other contacts, classified ads, employment agencies, and so forth. It may also eventually include those previously unknown to you, but revealed by your contacts or in the course of an interview. The model shows both the immediate supervisor and the executive responsible for the position, for the simple reason that either, or both, may be useful for direct approach. The "Expenses" column

JOB SEARCH CONTROL SHEET

Organization _____
Address _____
Phone _____
Date Search Began _____

Possible Contacts	Target Position(s)	Immediate Supervisor	Executive Supervisor	Expenses	Action

Information Checklist	Background Information:
☐ Annual Report	
☐ Employee Benefits	
☐ Promotion Policies	
☐ Training Programs	
☐ General Information	

FIGURE 4.1

JOB SEARCH CONTROL SHEET

Organization ABC Company, Inc.
Address 247 East 23rd Street
New York N.Y. 10021
Phone 212-681-5759
Date Search Began 12-2-80

Possible Contacts	Target Position(s)	Immediate Supervisor	Executive Supervisor	Expenses	Action
Robert Lukins (Friend of V.P. of Marketing) 213-456-7890	Market Research	Thomas A. Jones Sales Director (Secy- Carolyn Brown)	Diane Miller V.P. of Market- ing (Asst.- Andrew Smith)	12-2-80 Toll call to Lukins $3.69	12-2-80 Lukins will arrange lunch meeting with Miller 12-8-80 Lunch with Miller. Inter- view with Jones set for 12-10-80 12-10-80 Exum called to say he spoke to Jones and recommended me.
James Exum (Knows Sales Dir. through Sales Club.) 212-789-2456					

Background Information:

12-14-80 New marketing research planned for product under consideration. Will need additional staff.

12-16-80 Article in Wall St. Journal about plans for new
Denver plant. Copy in file.

Information Checklist:

☑ Annual Report
☑ Employee Benefits
☐ Promotion Policies
☐ Training Programs
☑ General Information

FIGURE 4.2

will show you at a glance just what each approach is costing, and will help you complete reimbursement forms for employers who invite you for interviews and offer to pick up your expenses. The "Action" column is an up-to-date progress report at each step. At the bottom of the control sheet, you'll find space to keep track of background information collected on the organization.

As you proceed with your campaign, you may want to revise column headings, add some, or attach another sheet for important data collected. If printed material or correspondence with contacts becomes voluminous, you may want to make up file folders, with the control sheets stapled to the inside cover. Remember, the form shown in Figure 4.2 is a model; it should serve only as a guide and, as in every other step of your search, it should be adapted to your individual needs.

Initially, you will have a large number of control sheets. In the final stages of your campaign, they will, by a process of elimination, constitute your "bible" of information on the half-dozen or so which seem to offer the best and most likely prospects for employment.

PEOPLE WHO CAN HELP

As you begin your search, by far the most important column on your control sheets is the first: possible contacts. We've all heard the phrase "It's not what you know, but who you know." Well, the "who" can seldom guarantee you a job and can never guarantee you will keep it once you're hired — only the "what" can do that. But a good contact *can* get your resume read by people who count, arrange for you to meet key executives, set up interviews, and most important of all, say just the right things about you to just the right people. Where will you find those contacts? In some places that may surprise you.

Let's start with the obvious: people you know. They may be friends, relatives, friends of relatives, the family doctor, lawyer, minister, rabbi or priest, your family's stockbroker, real estate broker, income tax specialist or banker, your librarian (who should be a good friend by now)—the list goes on and on. *Each one* is a potential source of contacts at your target organizations. *Talk to them.* Let everyone within earshot know you are interested in joining the ranks of the employed and which organizations interest you. You could find yourself in a well-paid position because your best friend knows the boss!

Another excellent source, although not so obvious, is alumni of your school. This rarely-used approach has much to recommend it. People have strong feelings for their alma maters, and a letter, even from a stranger, that asks for help for "a fellow graduate" is likely to get a friendly reception. You've already been directed to the alumni office as part of your organizational background investigations, and if you made contacts on that level, use them now to ask for a personal meeting to talk about employment possibilities. If the alumni organization has a directory, use it. Perhaps the placement office knows where to get names of alumni. Professors may know. Volunteer for a cause being sponsored by alumni and make contacts there.

You might even consider this unconventional approach if your school has a strong rival: writing to *its* alumni. If you learn that a graduate from the rival school holds an important position in one of your target organizations, write a letter which has as its theme: "Our schools competed on the football field, but now I would like to join your team. Please see me."

If you write to more than one person in the same company, be sure to send a carbon copy of each letter to the other person, with the standard notation "cc: Mr. (Ms.) _____" at the lower left margin. It exhibits professionalism and makes life easier for those you are contacting, since any action taken can be coordinated between two or among several. Also, if one of your letters is forwarded to the personnel department, they are immediately aware of all contacts. Finally, the recipients may talk to each other and decide that "one of us has to see this candidate." You get an interview, which is your goal in the first place.

Other very effective sources frequently are overlooked. Members of local community groups with which you and your family have been associated can be a goldmine of contacts. Worthwhile volunteer groups often include influential business leaders.

Leaders of veterans' organizations to which you or members of your family belong may point you to a valuable contact, or be contacts themselves.

The business editors of your local newspaper will have contacts that reach far beyond your own locality.

Anyone you meet socially who turns out to be interested in your career goals will be willing to help.

Local suppliers or clients of your target organizations are certain to know key people there.

Swap information with other students who you know are job hunting.

You can benefit from the experience of students who have

already landed a job with one of your targets. If they can give you a recommendation to someone in the firm, that will be a decided plus, since most organizations give preferential consideration to applicants referred by their own employees.

Once you have made a contact, ask for a private meeting to discuss in detail your qualifications (take along a resume) and your interest in the organization. This is where all that investigating will pay off. Show you have done your homework. Be prepared to discuss *enthusiastically* the background information you've gathered, the strength of the organization, its prestige, the direction(s) it is taking, and new areas it is opening up or exploring. Tell your contact why the organization appeals to you and how you feel you can contribute to its operation.

All this is a very positive indication that you not only *know* about the potential employer, but that you really *care* about working there. Most people respond very positively to that kind of approach. Remember, a person working for a firm usually feels pride and loyalty for it, and your demonstration of caring is in effect a compliment to the person you are talking to.

These all are ideas for putting a *human contact* approach into action. You may think of others. You should make those contacts as widespread as you possibly can. There is simply no way of telling where you may find that very important "who."

OTHER APPROACHES

At the same time you are building up good personal contacts, consider these methods which have worked for others in the past.

Direct Contact with Potential Employers

A very popular approach to job hunting is writing directly to potential employers in which you have an interest.

Contact each organization *selectively*. Write directly to the head of the functional division at which you are aiming (for example, a vice president of marketing, a director of research and development, the manager of the systems department). You may hit a bullseye! This technique bypasses other traditional approaches and could be a great time saver. The functional head knows all the present openings, who is to be replaced, transferred, or promoted, and the scope of future planning. If you are invited for an interview, you will be seen *selectively*, by the appropriate manager.

Perhaps the biggest disadvantage of this approach is that if your resume is misdirected, it may never get back into usual channels, that is, back to the personnel department. If it is put on hold, it may not be answered for a very long time. For that reason, it's a good idea to send a copy of your letter (along with your resume) to the personnel director.

Sometimes it pays to go straight to the top, especially in smaller organizations. Of course, a letter addressed to the president, marked "Personal," may not be read by the person addressed. It might be directed to other managers, or be sent directly to the personnel department. In any event, it travels with the imprint of someone in high office, and that can be an advantage. If the top executive does read it, then you have the attention of the single most important decision-maker.

Some applicants feel strong enough about their verbal persuasiveness to try securing an interview by phoning the person they would like to see. If you do so, here's a suggestion: call shortly before or after normal business hours. The person you've targeted may be there, possibly enabling you to avoid a secretary whose job may include screening out go-getters like you.

Some take the most direct approach of all: walking into the potential employer's office and asking for an interview. Stuart E. Eizenstat, who was President Carter's assistant for domestic affairs and policy, gives this advice: "It pays to make personal visits to prospective employers rather than just sending resumes. Whenever an employer has the choice between a known and unknown candidate, nine times out of ten the employer will choose the known candidate."

Of course, this approach demands a great deal of time, and not every employer rolls out the red carpet for walk-ins. But it's a method that a good number of people recommend, and one you should consider as you plan your job-finding strategy.

School Placement Office

If your school has a career center, you will want to make its placement office one of your first stops. At least one of your target organizations may have openings listed with it. It is also probable that you will come away with additions to your list of targets. This is one of the most important job lead sources for students, and the earlier you make yourself known to the placement office, the better your chances. They can save you considerable time, money, and frustration in developing contacts, because they have direct channels to interviewers.

As graduation nears and your goals crystalize, you'll find your placement office provides up-to-date job market data and on-campus interviews with employer recruiters. The value of on-campus interviews cannot be overstated. Employers who visit a college come with the hope of finding candidates they can refer for further interviews. What a wonderfully positive orientation! Unfortunately, schedules usually fill quickly and you sometimes can't get to see a representative from an employer high on your list. At most schools, when that happens the placement office gives the representative copies of employment credentials or placement service registration forms for those who could not get on the schedule. Because they are forms, all students appear to be similar. But you can help distinguish yourself by having your placement office attach a copy of your resume to the form. Follow up by sending the representative a letter with this theme: "Sorry I was unable to get on your campus schedule. I am especially interested in your company and am eager to see you during my spring break, when I plan to be in your city."

Many placement offices sponsor career fairs, where a large number of employers are represented in one place at one time, giving you an overall view of opportunities in a concentrated form. The placement office may also act as your personal employment agency, circulating your resume to potential employers, either directly or as part of "resume books;" this kind of help can lead to off-campus interviews. They can, in short, help you get to the job you want with the least possible expenditure of your time, effort, and money.

Recruiting Conferences

Attend recruiting conferences held on campus, and try to get to know the organizational representatives. One very good, little-used technique that can single you out from other candidates is a pre-conference letter (names of the representatives attending the conference are generally known to the placement office well in advance) expressing your interest in the organization and in a meeting when the recruiter is on campus. Even if your meeting with the representative should be unproductive, a follow-up note after the conference may keep you up front for future job exploration.

Classified Ads

The scanning of classified ads is a "must," especially in the Sunday newspapers. Look beyond the help-wanted section (although be sure to carefully comb that excellent resource). Some papers carry recruitment advertising in the business, financial, educational, or other sections. *The Wall Street Journal* runs a barrage of display and classified ads, especially on Tuesdays. Local newspapers in the geographic areas that interest you will have job openings. Your local library may contain an out-of-town newspaper file. Check the yellow pages to see if there is a local newsstand that sells them. If you must write or call for copies, your library will be able to furnish names and addresses from either the *Ayer Directory of Publications*, which lists news-papers by state and city, or *Working Press of the Nation*, newspaper edition, which is divided by area.

Do not overlook trade and professional magazines and journals, and specialty publications such as *Advance Job Listings*,[1] *Ad Search*,[2] or *Affirmative Action Register*.[3]

Personnel Departments

Generally, contacting personnel departments is not one of the more productive ways of securing interviews; they are flooded with an incredible volume of applications. Your resume exposure in many cases is limited to a quick, 15 to 60 second screening which may ignore or overlook your strong points. Because of personnel's desire to reduce turnover, lower training costs, and hold personnel prob-lems to a minimum, that department tends to quickly screen out many applicants whose resumes do not show the exact qualifications they are looking for. In other words, they are not as likely to take a chance on seeing you to try and determine your potential as would a management-level supervisor or division head. Not only that, they do not always know the organization's future plans or upcoming job openings. Management frequently waits to notify personnel of such developments after they are a fact, and if you have applied before then, you may have missed the boat.

Despite this dour reality, contact with personnel departments is a frequently used method by which many recent college grads find their first positions. If you do go this popular route, one way of standing out from the crowd is to phone the personnel director directly and ask for an interview, rather than write. That can be expensive if you live at a distance, but remember, it's hard for a per-sonnel director not to talk to someone who is paying for a costly call. If you have a good telephone personality, you will have made a good pre-interview impression, to be reinforced by your resume, which should be mailed along with a thank you letter before your visit. If your telephone personality is not very good, then a written request for an interview will probably serve you better. Make sure

---

[1] Advance Job Listings, P. O. Box 900, New York, N.Y. 10020
[2] Ad Search, Box 2083, Milwaukee, WI 53201
[3] Affirmative Action Register, 8356 Olive Blvd., St. Louis, MO 63132

the letter which accompanies your resume is an "action" letter. Ask for an *interview*, not "consideration." Keep the letter short, but make certain it has some evidence of your knowledge of the employer and your reasons for wanting to work there, as well as *the contributions you can make*. No one ever hired anyone because the applicant wanted "training" or "opportunity." People get hired because employers perceive that they can make contributions to the hiring organization, even if it means giving them extensive training first.

If you plan to be in the city to which your letter is addressed, on a certain day, or days, ask for a specific appointment. If you can afford to follow up such a request with a phone call, all the more effective.

Employment Agencies

Employment agencies can be a good job-hunting source if used wisely. If not, they can waste a lot of your valuable time by sending you to interviews that do not suit your needs or desires. If you do use employment agencies, do so intelligently by following these guidelines:

- Work with those agencies which specialize in the type of job you want, in the geographic area you desire.
- Visit the office to leave your resume, or mail it with a "selling" cover letter (see Chapter 7). Usually, they will give or mail an application form to you. Make copies of it before you return it, and send or bring along several copies of your resume.
- Maintain close contact. If you are assigned one person in the agency, develop that contact as you would a good friend.
- Report back on each job contact they furnish, and return their calls promptly.
- If appropriate, use them as your negotiator with an employer in relation to starting salary and possibly other employment terms.
- Do not visit agencies on Mondays or Fridays unless you have a specific appointment. On Mondays they're flooded with responses to ads they ran over the weekend, and on Fridays they're getting orders from clients and placing them in Sunday newspapers.
- Watch out for "bait and switch" tactics, where you are lured in for one job prospect but pressured into applying for another less desirable or less appropriate one. Keep your own requirements firmly in mind, but be flexible enough to realize that the agency may be acting in your best interests by directing you to a job not advertised. Just be sure that any such position meets your personal standards and goals.

- Be aware of the practice that a few agencies follow: "prospecting," or trying to get you to divulge all the places you have been for interviews. This gives them new potential clients to contact. Maintain confidentiality, sharing only information related to leads the particular agency gave you.
- Beware of a demand for "exclusive handling," which cuts you off from other employment agency contacts. Use as many as you wish, but recognize that there may be duplication, a time waster for them and you.

What costs are associated with employment agencies? In large urban centers, usually none. It is hard to find a sophisticated employer today in New York, Chicago, San Francisco, and other large cities, who will not pay the agency fee. At worst, some employers will ask you to pay the fee, but agree to reimburse you after a period of time, anywhere from three months to a year following employment. If an employment agency in a large city wants you to pay the fee, ask yourself whether this is the employer you want to work for, or the agency to use. In non-metropolitan areas, practices vary. Fees to applicants generally range from one week's to one month's salary. You can verify the propriety of a requested fee by checking with the state's or city's licensing or labor department.

"Career Services" Firms

You may wonder whether you should consider signing up with one of the companies specializing in helping applicants manage their job-hunting efforts. These firms typically offer their services in help-wanted sections of large-city newspapers, under titles such as Job Search Managers, Career Seeking Consultants, Job Hunting Marketers, and similar names. They charge fees for their services, which include resume preparation, mailings to potential employers, interview strategies, and career counsel. Their ads usually promise "no fee for evaluation interview," or "no cost or obligation to learn about our services." This does not mean, of course, that there is no fee for services they provide. While some graduates-to-be have been helped by these organizations, be warned that this is generally a very expensive approach to job seeking. If you follow the course set out in this book, you will perform most or all of such a firm's functions for yourself.

MAVERICK APPROACHES

Since the point of any approach is to single you out from other applicants, it would seem that unusual or maverick tactics would be to your advantage. *Sometimes* they are. For instance, someone looking for an opening in the field of advertising paraded up and down sidewalks in front of leading advertising agencies with a "sandwich board" displaying his qualifications and asking to be seen. He got three interviews, and a job. His approach worked because it showed, better than he could have "told," the imagination and creativity for which the advertising business is looking.

One young college graduate, working as a toll collector while looking for an entry-level position in packaged goods sales, posted a copy of her resume on her toll booth and handed out copies to drivers who reacted positively to her efforts. Result: six interviews, two offers, one happy candidate.

Here is an enterprising English major who attracted attention with a personalized t-shirt. Seen here with a copy of his local newspaper's help-wanted section, he also carried copies of his resume with him wherever he went.

An enthusiastic applicant — let's call him Sam Sharp — sent his resume to four department managers in one firm, attaching a thin strip of paper on which was typed: "Ask your personnel director whether Samuel J. Sharp is on the ball." Concurrently, he sent the personnel director a pink rubber ball on which he had written: "Samuel J. Sharp. On The Ball. Call 369-1234." Three of the four department managers called the personnel director to find out what was going on. The fourth sent him an inquiring memo. All wanted to know more about Sam. Needless to say, the personnel director, whose own curiosity was aroused, called Sam in. That's one way to generate interest from a busy personnel department!

Students at five schools with real estate and construction management programs pooled their efforts and worked exhibit space donated by the National Association of Home Builders at their convention. The students handed out brochures on their colleges' programs, and had piles of student resumes at hand. Conventioneers responded with enthusiasm; on-campus interviewing of graduates-to-be went up dramatically.

Raymond D. Reed, dean of the College of Architecture and Environmental Design, Texas A&M University, found a position in this unconventional way: "I was once seeking a job in a strange city with no personal or professional references. I went to a prestigious architectural firm who, I had been told, was looking for a designer. The principal of the firm admitted that he needed a designer but had no idea of my abilities. I had no examples of my work and no personal references. I offered to work for one week at the end of which he could then inform me whether he wished me to continue to work for him and, if so, at what salary. Obviously, during the week I did my best, and at the end of the week I was offered a permanent position at a more-than-fair salary."

Had these applicants been seeking jobs with staid, ultra-conservative employers, their approaches probably would have failed. The trick in using unusual or gimmicky approaches is to be sure they fit the situation. If you have solid qualifications, and can present them with humor or style that is appropriate, you may well come out the happy recipient of a job offer. Just be sure you know when to stop being a maverick (after you've gained an interview) and start being a serious contender for the job.

WHEN TO START
YOUR JOB SEARCH

The best time to apply for a job varies among employers but, generally, you should start organizing your campaign a minimum of five or six months before graduation. If you are seeing on-campus recruiters, you don't have to give timing much thought, as the placement office does it for you. If you are planning a trip to a particular city or region and expect to be there several days with the hope of seeing potential employers, get your letters out a full month in advance to give both them and you time to set things up properly.

When to start your campaign is often determined by factors outside your control. For example, teaching jobs usually open prior to January and September. In general, job hirings come to a standstill at the end of December, but right after the new year is often a very active hiring time. Many employers start their formal training programs in June. Plant expansions, new construction, new products, and new markets opened, all signal possible job openings and should be acted on immediately. To pinpoint hiring patterns in an area, visit or contact the nearest office of the State Employment Job Service or regional office of the Federal Bureau of Labor Statistics (both listed in your telephone directory).

Remember, too, that it is sometimes difficult to follow up on jobs during summer vacation periods and, for many executives in the north, during December, when winter vacations are popular.

JOB-SEEKING IS HARD WORK

No one ever said that finding a good job was easy. Application of energy and effective techniques is a *must* for the vast majority of entry-level job seekers. "Hang everlastingly on to the job of trying to secure a job," says William G. Dunn, vice president-publisher of *U. S. News & World Report.* "So many young persons tend to get discouraged very easily if the world does not come together for them within a five-day period." Earl G. Graves, publisher of *Black Enterprise Magazine,* has a similar perspective: "If there is a 'magic' ingredient, I would call it persistence."

Obviously, no individual is likely to attempt all the approaches described in this chapter. But by considering each you will have the ammunition you need to develop the most comfortable fit for yourself, possibly combining two or more when appropriate, or pursuing several individually in sequence or concurrently. William May, dean of the Graduate School of Business, New York University, formerly American Can Company's chairman of the board, emphasizes this point when he says: "In my judgment, most individuals are too limited in the search they undertake—they contact too few companies and put too many eggs in one basket. I believe in the adage that the more lines you have in the water, the more likely you will catch fish—the more companies you contact the more likely you will find the best fit to begin a career."

IN BRIEF

This chapter has discussed your personal marketing strategy, including what information you will need about target employers; how to get it; who can help you with a "human contact" approach; other useful approaches; and the timing of your campaign.

Your next step is a crucial one: preparing that all-important written document, a resume, as a key step in reaching and impressing potential employers.

5

Resumes I:
Preparing
to Sell Yourself
on Paper

Having gone through the all-important process of plotting an effective campaign to win the job you want, you are ready to pitch into the long and exacting process of actually getting it.

Essentially, you are faced with a selling job. Everything you know about yourself must be packaged and marketed so that the product you present to employers — *You* — will have as much sales appeal as you can give it. The package is called a *resume* — a written document revealing the work-related history and qualifications you have to offer.

"Hunting a job is a marketing experience," says Sid Bernstein, chairman of the executive committee for Crain Communications. "What you are selling is yourself — your ability and personality. And your marketing effort is more difficult than most because you must first locate a potential market — some place which wants and needs someone with a particular set of knowledge and skills — and you must sell yourself as the one possessing those attributes. So don't be bashful . . . advertise your availability as widely as possible, and make use of any legitimate means of getting consideration."

PREPARING TO WRITE
YOUR RESUME

Much of the labor of resume writing never appears in the final product. But without it, that product may be nothing more than a poorly organized piece of paper that is among the first to be discarded by screeners.

Your first order of business is to reduce to writing everything job-related you know about yourself. This is no small task, but it is absolutely essential. The quickest, easiest way to do this is to start with worksheets on which you can make the first entries of your qualifications by category. Begin with the worksheets shown in Figures 5.1, 5.2, and 5.3, which cover education, work experience, and personal interests and skills. Once completed, your worksheets should provide a detailed profile from which to ferret out the positive aspects in each area you will want to stress in your resume, as well as to prepare yourself for interviews. They should stimulate a self-examination that will enable you to compile your own inventory of all the training, experience, and interests that make up the *You* product you will be marketing.

Nothing is too trivial to be included in this initial, overall look at yourself. Organization, at this point, consists solely of categorizing the mass of information from which you will select what is relevant to your job search. Don't worry just now if some of your summer jobs seems inconsequential or your interest in making home movies seems to have no bearing on your future career. Furthermore, polished wording is of no importance on the worksheets. The point is to *get it all down* so that when the time comes for making choices, you will have before you a complete picture.

You may find it helpful to go over your worksheet with parents or friends, since they may be able to spot omissions that have slipped your mind.

TAKING A CLOSE LOOK
AT YOURSELF

In addition to the three worksheets, your personal inventory should include answers to two important questions: "Who am I?" and "What are my assets?"

"Who am I?" is a question almost trite in today's "me"-oriented society. Yet, in this business of beginning a life's work, it must be answered. Only by bringing a sense of order into your sometimes

```
EDUCATION WORKSHEET


COLLEGE

Name _____

Year Graduated _____

Degree _____

Major _____

Minor _____

Awards/Honors _____

GRADUATE OR PROFESSIONAL SCHOOL

Name _____

Year Graduated _____

Degree _____

Major _____

Minor _____

Awards/Honors _____

OTHER EDUCATION

Institution _____

Degree/Certificate _____

Course of Study _____


Institution _____

Degree/Certificate _____

Course of Study _____
```

FIGURE 5.1

SCHOLARSHIPS

Source, Nature, Amount _____

Source, Nature, Amount _____

Source, Nature, Amount _____

Assistantship/Fellowship _____

Assistantship/Fellowship _____

EVALUATION

Favorite Subjects _____

Reason _____

Least Favorite Subjects _____

Reason _____

Best Grades _____

Poorest Grades _____

Special Achievements _____

INVOLVEMENTS

Extra-Curricular Activities _____

On-Campus Memberships _____

Professional Memberships _____

Alumni Activities _____

PLANS FOR FUTURE TRAINING/STUDY

Subject _____

Why Interested _____

When Planned _____

MISCELLANEOUS

Licenses/Certifications _____

Published Articles/Books _____

Attendance at Professional Meetings/Conferences _____

Special Projects _____

FIGURE 5.1 (continued)

WORK EXPERIENCE WORKSHEET

Employer _____

Dates _____

Position _____

Duties/Responsibilities (Did performance indicate aptitudes of intelligence,

    numerical ability, verbal facility, leadership, decision-making, special skills,

    supervision?) _____

_____

Knowledge Acquired _____

Achievement(s) _____

Employer _____

Dates _____

Position _____

Duties/Responsibilities (Did performance indicate aptitudes of intelligence,

    numerical ability, verbal facility, leadership, decision-making, special skills,

    supervision?) _____

_____

Knowledge Acquired _____

Achievement(s) _____

Employer _____

Dates _____

Position _____

Duties/Responsibilities (Did performance indicate aptitudes of intelligence,

    numerical ability, verbal facility, leadership, decision-making, special skills,

    supervision?) _____

_____

FIGURE 5.2

Knowledge Acquired _____

Achievement(s) _____

Employer _____

Dates _____

Position _____

Duties/Responsibilities (Did performance indicate aptitudes of intelligence,

   numerical ability, verbal facility, leadership, decision-making, special skills,

   supervision?) _____

_____

Volunteer Work (charities, civic, welfare, religious) _____

_____

Internships _____

_____

Entrepreneurial Activities _____

_____

_____

FIGURE 5.2 (continued)

PERSONAL INTERESTS & SKILLS WORKSHEET

Activity _____

How Long? _____

Competence _____

Application to Field of Interest _____

Activity _____

How Long? _____

Competence _____

Application to Field of Interest _____

Activity _____

How Long? _____

Competence _____

Application to Field of Interest _____

Activity _____

How Long? _____

Competence _____

Application to Field of Interest _____

Activity _____

How Long? _____

Competence _____

Application to Field of Interest _____

FIGURE 5.3

Activity _____

How Long? _____

Competence _____

Application to Field of Interest _____

Activity _____

How Long? _____

Competence _____

Application to Field of Interest _____

Activity _____

How Long? _____

Competence _____

Application to Field of Interest _____

Special Skills (Typing, steno, office machines, computer languages, statistics,
    foreign language(s), photography, writing, counseling, leadership, etc.)

_____

_____

_____

_____

_____

FIGURE 5.3 (continued)

conflicting needs and expectations can you hope to make the right choices.

Your individual personality is the sum of inherited traits, cultural and social conditioning, and your self-image. Your personal inventory should list your personality traits as you know them. Be as objective as you can. While only *you* can make a complete list, the following will serve to get your self-evaluation off the ground:

- Are you outgoing and friendly, or reserved and shy?
- Are you basically a "loner," or are you happiest doing things with a group?
- How important to you is prestige? Power? Social position? Money?
- Do you want to join the ranks of the professions (doctor, lawyer, and so on), or do you want to be a part of the business, government, or educational communities?
- Do you have your heart set on living and working in a specific geographic location? Is where you are more important to you than what you do?
- Are you drawn to service-oriented activities which offer more in personal satisfaction than in monetary rewards?
- Do you work best under pressure, or at a more relaxed pace? Is setting your own pace for yourself especially important to you?
- Do you enjoy challenges?
- Are you assertive, or do you prefer to follow the lead of others?
- Do you like to travel, or is an unchanging home base important to you?
- Have you made your decision clearly and unequivocally to get a job rather than continue on with higher education? Will you want to pursue further studies, part-time, while working?
- Do you have a vision of what you want your life's work to achieve, or are you still in the exploratory or undecided stage?

Arriving at honest answers to questions such as these is no easy matter. It cannot be accomplished in a few minutes, but as you dig deep within yourself to discover what really motivates you and just what your psychological needs are, you will begin to make some of the broader choices on which later, more specific, ones must be based. For example, if a prestigious title really matters to you, then recognize that a less prestigious job, even if it pays more, would bring you less personal satisfaction. Or, if the money you earn represents your true worth in your own eyes, then you can forego titles in favor of money in the bank. You will be able to decide if a social service job, for instance, would satisfy a desire to make a contribution or merely lead to frustration because you were not earning as much as you could elsewhere. By acknowledging that inner longing to live in a certain region, you can understand that a job elsewhere, whatever the pay, is not going to compensate for not being there. If you have a clear vision of your life's work, you may feel that nothing else will bring the same satisfaction as associating yourself with leaders in that field, no matter what the beginning position.

By crystalizing your "wants," you will lay the foundation for that career you are beginning to build. You will be in a position to weigh options and alternatives and set priorities. You can measure the relative importance of tangibles (money and things) against intangibles (pleasure and psychological rewards). With a clear picture in mind of what it is you want, you can better set about the task of getting it.

The question "What are my assets?" is answered by listing the skills, education, and experience you have already acquired which are marketable.

Definable skills should include everything you can perform adequately. List them all, from technical skills (for example, has your interest in amateur radio broadcasting or home movie making resulted in wiring, lighting, or production skills?) to cultural skills such as music, creative writing, or painting. These are the things you can do, and any one — or all of them — could be transferable to a job situation.

Review your education in detail, including any recognition you have achieved through honors, awards, or leadership positions in the academic area, plus any specific knowledge gained from such activities as project design and participation.

List all the courses you have completed. Some courses which you consider inconsequential at the moment may well turn out to be applicable to your final job choice. Search your records and memory for all forms of academic recognition, since they can serve as valuable clues to an aptitude you might otherwise overlook. Generalized courses like human relations and communication skills are applicable in almost all career areas. Indeed, while the content of a specific job is usually learned after you have begun work, the valuable transferable skills of getting along with people and effectively communicating with them are very important to employers since they often spell the difference between success and failure.

Apply the same sort of scrutiny to specific knowledge you've picked up from working on school projects. A lab project many times enhances your background on the subject under study. Sociological or historical research projects involve techniques and information which increase your expertise beyond the scope of normal classroom activity. Remember, this is an inventory of *all* the educational benefits you have garnered thus far.

As for work experience, even if it is extremely limited at this time, write it all down. In the humblest part-time job, you have been exposed to at least some of the organizational structure, pressures, and human-relations aspects which exist at all levels of the work world. If you've worked as a volunteer for charity, you've seen first hand the structure required to arrive at a desired goal. Volunteer work in a political campaign, even if confined to door-to-door solicitation for contributions, will have sharpened your awareness of the techniques of dealing with people.

All of these considerations are a part of the total *You* picture, so spend the time and effort to uncover every possible asset you now possess.

> The resume is essentially a piece of advertising copy, a marketing device through which an individual presents himself/herself in the marketplace. As such, one should employ the tenets that are applied to good advertising copy, that is, accentuate the positive; eliminate the negative (or at least downplay it); be brief and concise; use a graphic approach that highlights what is most dramatic and important in your background.
>
> LEE GURTIN
> DIRECTOR OF PLACEMENT AND CAREER PLANNING
> GRADUATE SCHOOL OF BUSINESS
> UNIVERSITY OF PITTSBURGH

WHAT YOU SHOULD PUT IN YOUR RESUME

What should you put in a resume? *Everything that will help the screener screen you in!* Everything that will say to the reader: "Here is an applicant who is not like every other applicant. Here is someone who may become a viable candidate for the open job."

To determine what information will accomplish this, put yourself in the employer's shoes; think about the job you want from the viewpoint of the person doing the hiring. Analyze your objective for requirements of education, training, experience, and personal traits, as though you were preparing a "help-wanted" advertisement. Then, match your qualifications with those the job is likely to demand. In other words, let your resume package tell the employer specifically what your product has to offer *in terms of the needs to be filled.* Even if you aren't aware of *specific* job openings at the time of your application, by now you should be on intimate terms with the *general* qualifications that can be adapted to openings in your field, as well as any special qualifications you gathered along the way to the job market.

In all cases, your resume must include these basics:

1. Identification (Name, address and telephone number)
2. Job Objective (A brief, concise statement of what you are looking for)
3. Education (Colleges attended, degrees and major, with a brief statement covering any special emphasis in your major/minor or any significant special training courses or seminars)
4. Work Experience (Duties and most important accomplishments, length of employment, with special emphasis on work experience appropriate to your career field. Susan Shaffer's resume, Figure 5.4, demonstrates how these first four sections can be clearly and effectively organized.)
5. Special Qualifications (Extra-curricular activities, honors or awards received, skills, publications, languages, travel, military service, professional memberships, licenses related to job interest, willingness to relocate. The second page of Rhonda Petrovsky's resume, Figure 5.5, is an excellent example of how a highly involved, outstanding student presented her extra-curricular activities and honors. These sections convey her demonstrated leadership qualities, as well.)
6. Personal Interests (At least three — fewer, and you may appear shallow — and not more than six, seven, or eight — lest you appear to be spread too thin — to humanize the resume. Consider the value of demonstrating varied interests, such as intellectual, physical, social, and cultural.)

Later on in this chapter you will find specific suggestions and guidelines for these various sections, to help you construct an effective resume.

WHAT YOU SHOULD
LEAVE OUT

Omit those things that are likely to cause an interviewer to eliminate your resume from consideration. Specifics follow.

The bald-faced entry "Unemployed" has no place in a resume. As a soon-to-be or recent grad, it will be taken for granted that you are not presently employed, at least not full time. In addition, there

SUSAN SHAFFER

Present Address:

4105 Pine Street #6
Philadelphia, PA. 19104
215-222-0311

Permanent Address:

1000 No. Northlake Drive
Hollywood, FL. 33019
305-925-0653

OBJECTIVE

A management training position in sales which will enable me to use my organizational, administrative and human relations skills.

EDUCATION

THE UNIVERSITY OF PENNSYLVANIA, Philadelphia, PA.
Candidate for Bachelor of Arts in Urban Studies, May, 1981. Concentration in Political Science. Wharton School course work includes Decision Science, Accounting, Economics and Statistics.
Scholastic Average: 3.3/4.0 Average in Major: 3.5
Activities: Active member of Penn Union Council, Penn Political Union, Spring Fling Committee 1980 - 81, Blood Donor Club (1979), Womens Intramural Sports

THE UNIVERSITY OF FLORIDA, Gainesville, FL. 9/77 - 6/78
Courses studied in College of Liberal Arts.
Scholastic Average: 3.8
Honors and Activities: Dean's List (1978) Assistant Coordinator for Dormitory Activities housing 700 students.

EXPERIENCE

Concession Manager, Spring Fling Committee, University of Pennsylvania, 1980 - 81. Subcontracted with Refreshment Company to sell at annual Festival for 20,000 people. Wrote and implemented contract.

Student Intern, Commission on Human Relations, Philadelphia, PA. 1/80 - 5/80. Interviewed clients and referred to appropriate Commission Member, visited clients at their residence, personally assisted those with immediate problems of discrimination in housing, employment and public accomodations.

LBJ Student Intern, United States Congress, Washington, D.C. 7/12/79 - 8/30/79. Performed legislative research, corresponded with constituents and reported on various Senate hearings.

Assistant Art Director, City of Hollywood Recreation Department, Hollywood, FL. 6/78 - 8/78. Directed art instruction for 85 children in Summer Day Care Camp, maintained an accurate account of materials and supplies and assisted in the coordination of other activities.

Sales Clerk, Lory's Fashions, Hollywood, FL. 9/76 - 1/77. Sold clothing and accessories in womens sportswear store.

Other work experience includes waitress, secretary and own financial ventures.

PERSONAL DATA

Born July 14, 1959. Single. Excellent health. Travelled extensively throughout the United States and Europe. Interests include dancing, swimming and tennis. Knowledge of Spanish. Familiarity with APL and SPSS programming.

FIGURE 5.4

COLLEGE ACTIVITIES

University of Tennessee Ad Club (American Advertising Federation), 1976-79
    Publicity Chairperson, 1978-79
District Seven AAF College Representative to the District Seven Board of Directors
    (Student on the Board) 1978-79
District Seven AAF Collegiate Club Officers' Workshop Coordinator, 1979
The Greater Knoxville Advertising Club, member 1978-79
The University of Tennessee University Council, student member, 1978-79
College of Communications Dean's Student Advisory Committee, 1978-79
Marketing Research Assistant, 1978-79
Student Government Association (SGA):
    Director of Communications, 1977-78
    SGA Screening Committee, 1977-79; Chairperson, 1978-79
    Editor of The Student Advocate, a quarterly newspaper for SGA, 1977-78
Zeta Tau Alpha Sorority (ZTA):
    Executive Board Member, 1976
    Panhellenic Council, 1976   Rush Counselor, 1977
    Co-editor of the Greek Survival Kit, a study of life after college, 1978

COLLEGE HONORS

Chancellor's Citation for "Extraordinary Professional Promise," awarded by
    Jack E. Reese, Chancellor of The University of Tennessee, 1979
"Most Outstanding Advertising Student," awarded by The Greater Knoxville
    Advertising Club, 1979
District Seven AAF Student Advertising Campaigns Competition, Winner, 1979
National AAF Student Advertising Campaigns Competition, First Place Winner, 1979
Senior Collegiate Direct Mail/Marketing Institute - Scholarship recipient, 1978
    (one of 34 advertising and marketing students nationwide awarded
     this scholarship for academic and extra-curricular achievements,
     as well as professional aptitude)
Scripps-Howard Myron G. Chambers Scholarship recipient, 1978
Advertising Scholastic Fund, Scholarship recipient, 1979
Phi Eta Sigma Honor Society
Gamma Beta Phi Honor Society
Phi Kappa Phi Honor Society
Kappa Tau Alpha Communications Honor Society
Alpha Delta Sigma Advertising Honor Society
Omicron Delta Kappa National Leadership and Honor Fraternity
Mortar Board National Honor Society - PRESIDENT, 1978-79
Dean's List, with High and Highest Honors for 12 quarters at UT

PERSONAL DATA

Date of birth: May 7, 1957; health: excellent; height: 5'6"; weight: 130
marital status: single; interests: snow skiing, horseback riding, scuba
diving, photography, performing arts.

FIGURE 5.5

is an unconscious, very virulent discrimination in the marketplace against the unemployed, probably based on the presumption that there is something wrong with you if you are not working. Even though this is not quite so strong when it comes to recent graduates seeking entry-level jobs, the word "unemployed" should be avoided.

Do not show grade averages unless you have at least a 3.2 on a 4.0 scale. You are free, of course, to arrange the presentation of your grades in ways more favorable than a cumulative grade-point average (GPA) might show. For example, if your overall average is 2.9, but the average of courses in your major is 3.4, you might list the latter in the "Education" section of your resume (always indicate the maximum grade, for example, 3.4/4.0, if you are on a four-point scale). Or suppose you did not do as well your first two years as you did while a junior and senior. Assuming your program followed a typical sequence, you could state "Advanced Courses GPA, 3.5/4.0." The same goes for graduate school versus undergraduate—there is no requirement that you list grades for both. You can select one or the other, both, or neither. Remember, carrying your GPA to one decimal place gives you the right to list a 3.55 as 3.6.

As for class standing, list it only if you are in at least the top one-third. A major survey revealed that better than three out of every five employers feel grades play an important role, and fully 97 percent consider them of some relevance. Unless yours are especially good, let your transcript speak for itself, if it is requested following an interview.

Some information is just plain nonsense on a resume, such as your social security number, where you were born, your spouse's name, and your health status. (In the case of health, "excellent," is a cliché, and anything else, even "good," raises questions.) It is even highly questionable that age and marital status belong in a resume. If there is a reader bias on either score, there is no point in eliminating yourself before you have an opportunity to overcome it in a personal interview. However, if you feel comfortable having them shown in your resume, by all means include them. The point is, at the time of screening, every single item in your resume should be as much a known "positive" as you can possibly determine.

Never mention salary expectations in a resume. You could be undervaluing or overpricing yourself without knowing it. Leave this kind of delicate negotiation for later in the hiring process. It is usually not an appropriate subject for discussion until after a firm offer has been made.

Unless you are applying for a position as a model or entertainer, or in a highly creative field, your best bet is to not have a photograph

of yourself. Some screeners consider use of a photo very unsophisticated. Why run the risk that your resume's reader may react negatively to a facial expression your mother would absolutely adore?

References also are not usually relevant at the resume stage.
They can become important after you have been interviewed and are
a serious candidate for a job. Exceptions would be a reference whose
name is a household word or those meaningful in your career field,
in-company contacts, and the like. Or, if it is an especially well-
written reference, related to your career objective, you might work
it into your resume (see Miriam Suchoff's resume in Appendix C).

As for the trite phrase "References Furnished on Request,"
leave it off. Of course you'll furnish references if they're asked for,
so why state the obvious? You should be sure, however, to have
names, addresses, and telephone numbers with you when you go in
for an interview.

Reference letters are a somewhat different story. If you are
already working, letters from former or current full-time employers
usually should not be attached to a resume. They are often considered to be a clue that the writers are hoping not to be contacted
personally regarding your work performance. If you have not worked
full-time, however, and have especially laudatory epistles from professors, summer employers of note (not the village fruit store), or
from the military, you may wish to attach them.

Finally, race, religion, politics, or personal finances are *not*
resume material, regardless of how you word them.

In summary, your resume should not give the scanner any
reason *not* to interview you. Give yourself every break possible by
including only pertinent, positive data.

HOW YOU CAN "HUMANIZE" YOUR RESUME

It is those "Special Qualifications" and "Personal Interests" noted as
necessary on your resume that can often reach out and establish
human contact with the screener.

Suppose, for example, you have been active in campus theater
productions or the college debate team. That experience may, on
the face of it, seem to be unrelated to your value as a future employee. However, in some career fields, the employer may put a high
value on an ability to think on your feet or on the personal
"presence" necessary in stage work. In those instances, you take on
another dimension when a screener spots your experience. In other

words, you begin to emerge as an individual — a desirable potential employee — just from information which appears on a printed page.

In the same way, special honors or awards — in whatever area — can help spotlight you as exceptional or, at least, out of the ordinary. Hobbies or cultural interests may also strike a responsive chord.

Be sure, though, to include only those special qualifications and personal interests which are significant to *You*. Do not include casual, trivial, or passing fancies. Again, it is important to *Be Yourself*. After all, if a recruiter picks up on any one of these humanizing factors, you must be able to follow through with sincere, intelligent, enthusiastic backup.

IMPACT FOR YOUR RESUME

Because your resume is a selling device, you must emphasize your accomplishments and achievements if you want to stand out among the many applicants with whom you're competing.

An excellent approach to this process is proposed by a communications/marketing consultant who previously taught at Michigan State. Dr. Charles R. Mauldin says: "Students often assume that there is a right way to write and organize a resume. One way. And that they will fare poorly if they do not follow the one right form. I guess that should not surprise. They have been through years of filling out tests and forms for which there are right and wrong answers. And many have collected one or more examples of resumes that are pretty much alike. But it is best to think of the resume as having to persuade a prospective employer to invite you in for an interview . . . it is a selling piece, not just an information piece."

Dr. Mauldin had his students prepare a "brag sheet," making a list of claims they thought should be important to an employer. Then they wrote down under each claim every bit of support they could think of, not just from academic life, but from extracurricular activities, jobs, hobbies, volunteer assignments, and the like.

What kinds of claims did they support? Intelligence. Leadership. Maturity. Innovation. Loyalty. Sound judgment. Devotion to task. Dozens of others. The "brag sheet" is as important as the education, work experience, and personal interests worksheets. All should be combined to develop a positive, accomplishment-oriented resume.

Resume writing time is not the time to prove how modest you can be. Remember that accomplishments and achievements sell, and selling yourself is your primary goal.

PUTTING YOUR RESUME
TOGETHER

With your worksheets and lists complete, you are ready for the next step: the actual writing of your resume. At this stage, you must pay close attention to such finer points as careful selection of facts, a thoughtful choice of words, and a decision as to format or formats. Some job-seekers find the task of transferring data from a personal inventory to a resume so formidable that they turn to professionals to do the job for them. The best advice is: *write it yourself*! It is *your* resume, and it is important that the finished product be your own expression of yourself. Screeners are quick to spot the professionally written resume, and many times just as quick to toss it aside.

To take some of the fear out of the writing process, let's look at a few of the mechanics which will help you. Keep in mind that you are trying to make a strong impression in the first few seconds your resume is scanned, then consider how the following guidelines will help you do that.

Style

Just as telegrams are often more effective than lengthy letters, so a resume written in a fast and easy "Western Union literary" style will get your message across faster and with more force than a wordy, autobiographical approach. Telegrams use short sentences or phrases. So should your resume — with simple, *positive* wording. For example, contrast "As salesman in my summer job at XYZ Men's Store, I was made temporary manager of the sportswear department" with "Promoted from salesman to summer manager of sportswear department for XYZ Men's Store." "Promoted" is far stronger than "I was made," and the shorter phrasing makes for quicker reading. Here are some action-oriented, positive words which will be useful in writing your resume:

administered	developed
analyzed	established
budgeted	implemented
conducted	improved
coordinated	increased (sales, output, etc.)
created	influenced
designed	investigated (research)
directed	maintained

52

managed	produced
operated	reduced (costs, time, etc.)
organized	scheduled
planned	supervised
prepared	trained
presented	wrote

Placement of Information
Selective placement is a way to strengthen your resume. If you are short on job-related work experience, heavy on education, list your academic accomplishments first, with emphasis on any honors. On the other hand, if you have significant work experience, that should appear near the top of your resume and be given more space than educational credits.

Abbreviations
Better not to use any at all unless they are extremely common (such as "Inc."). Otherwise, they can create confusion: is "Eng." English or Engineering? Does "#" mean number or pounds? And, while many screeners may wonder just what "d/b/a"[1] or "a/k/a"[2] mean, you can bet they won't take the time to find out!

Grammar
Misspellings and poor grammar can land your resume in the rejection pile. If you are uncertain about either, *be sure to check it out*. And while you're at it, take another look at punctuation. A misplaced comma can produce a wrong interpretation.

Currency
Resume reviewers often react to outdated resumes as being indicators of applicant carelessness or inattention to details. That certainly will not do you any good. You can keep your resume up-to-date by carefully wording entries involving dates. For example, avoid "Will graduate in May, 19xx," because your resume is dated as soon as May arrives. All you need do in that case is enter your graduation date, even though it is in the future. The reader will understand that you are still in school. Similarly, avoid phrases which refer to expectations and pending or future events or circumstances.

[1] "doing business as"
[2] "also known as"

Length

Most experts advise confining your resume to one page if at all possible, not more than two. Certainly it is true that a single page can be more quickly scanned than two, and in the case of most entry-level applicants, a single page usually is sufficient. It also forces you to be concise. However, if you have had a lot of experience or training that will significantly enhance your chances of getting an interview, put it in, regardless of the space required. Remember, though, that every entry should be as short and as punchy as possible. Go to the extra page only after you have written and rewritten every element into its most effective form.

ITEM BY ITEM

With the above guidelines firmly in mind and your personal inventory worksheets at hand, you can begin the first draft.

Heading

Do not use one. A resume is obviously a resume and does not need to be labeled as such.

Identification

Your name, address, and telephone number are the only identification necessary. If you show both a home and school address and telephone number, be sure you make clear which is which.

Placement of your identity will depend on the format you use. Centering it at the top is generally effective and creates a pleasing look, but flush to the left margin is popular and certainly acceptable.

If your resume runs to two pages or more, be sure your name appears at the top of each page so they can be easily reunited if separated.

Job Objective

Consider this type of vacuous verbiage, too often used: "A challenging and demanding position of responsibility, offering me training and advancement, with a goal-oriented organization." That does not mean a thing in specific terms. You are asking the reader to decide what kind of work you should apply for; it wastes valuable space; it implies concern for your own self-interests rather than contributions you might make to the employer; and it diverts the screener's attention from whatever you might have specifically to offer. It certainly does not help make you an appealing candidate.

Another type of objective often seen, but harmful to its authors, is the objective which covers too many possibilities and focuses on what the writer wants from the company, rather than ability, skills, and qualities being offered. Typically it reads something like this: "To obtain a management position in marketing, production, personnel, or purchasing, in a company which offers opportunity for growth and advancement." Applicants with objectives such as this are called in for interviews far less often than those who construct meaningful, employer-related statements such as those explained below.

Heed the helpful advice of Robert L. Van Wey, college relations associate for the Brunswick Corporation: "The ideal candidate for entry-level management positions is one who states the functional area (that is, sales, accounting, finance, and so on) that he/she wishes to be considered for and presents credentials that demonstrate interest in and commitment to the field. If the candidate simply applies for any position, or a 'management' job, the recruiter is placed in the most difficult position of making a career decision for the candidate. With the cost of employing and training an individual being substantial, the recruiter will be hesitant to consider the candidate further."

Your resume objective should relate generally to your immediate goal, while mentioning what you have to offer. For example, "To utilize analytical abilities and previous work experience in a managerial finance or accounting position."

Kenneth B. Hoyt, director, Career Education, U.S. Department of Education, says: "You need to be able to demonstrate to an employer two things. One is your ability to do a specific job that will make money for the employer very shortly after you are hired. The second is your potential for contributing to the larger goals of the organization."

Because the objective is frequently the first thing read on the resume (even before the identification section), its importance cannot be overstated. A poorly or naively written objective can be a turnoff for a resume reader, and that means no invitation for an interview. Plan your objective statement very carefully. In doing so, consider these examples of objectives which worked well for their authors:

- "An entry-level management position which requires utilization of analytical and interpersonal skills. Ultimately to become a progressive integrative manager from experiences in organizational planning, human resources development, finance and management policy."

- "The opportunity to apply my chemical engineering education and research-oriented interests in a consumer-oriented manufacturing company."
- "A position in real estate management or development utilizing financial and communication skills."
- "A career with a consulting or technologically based firm which combines marketing and strategic planning skills."
- "Responsibility for organizational development, including implementation of corporate change, improving productivity and quality of work life, making maximum utilization of computer-based information systems, integrating corporate/community concerns."
- "Consultant to organizations and industry in corporate strategy, government policy and liaison, and facilities location analysis. Strong interest in the international business environment."
- "Seeking a position in accounting management, financial administration and/or credit and collections, utilizing my graduate education and practical part-time field experience."
- "Advertising account management utilizing marketing orientation (internship experience in developing consumer product marketing plans); management, organizational and leadership skills (gained through academic and practical work experience); achievement under pressure (honors graduate while working full and part time)."
- "Hardworking and highly responsible MBA seeks challenging opportunity in the marketing/marketing research department of a consumer-goods marketer."

Education

Do not list your high school; it's your college degree that will interest employers. If you earned honors or were class valedictorian, mention so in a separate resume section which might be called, for example, "Academic Achievements," or "Honors and Awards."

If you have attended more than one college, list only the degree-granting school unless a prior school is more prestigious or of a specialized nature that is significant in your career field.

If you have little or no work experience, punch up educational qualifications by referring to your college catalog for short, terse course descriptions. Tightly written by experts, they usually include a statement of how they apply to your career field.

Perhaps even more important is a point clearly expressed by Howard Toy, director of personnel for the Smithsonian Institution: "How can I get any experience if no one will hire me? is a frequent lament among young people looking for an entry level job. Truly a Catch-22 situation — if it were true. I happen to believe that it is not true. Think about your hobbies, your religious or other voluntary activities, the offices and memberships you have held in various clubs and organizations, and the various research projects you have had throughout the college years. All these activities add up to experience. Think about it and you may be surprised that much of it may be relevant to the entry job you are looking for. Don't sell yourself short. You have a lot more experience than you first realize."

Extra-Curricular Activities

These can be very impressive, especially if they demonstrate interest in your career field or show managerial skills, such as leadership or organizational ability. If you can show these qualities, list extra-curricular activities immediately following the educational section. In the functional format (see Chapter 6), they may be more usefully employed under one or more of your functional headings.

Work Experience

If your work experience is appropriate to the job for which you are applying, be sure it is prominently placed and takes up more space than anything else on your resume. Stress significant functions and *accomplishments.*

Use the strongest action verbs and phrases good conscience will permit, and try to arrange job elements with the most important duties and accomplishments first. Stress transferable skills such as dependability and initiative.

You do not need a great deal of detail about previous employers. What you got out of the experience is what is important to an interviewer. Dr. Larry Smith, director of placement and career planning at the Graduate School of Management, University of California, Los Angeles, brings home the point: "What employers are interested in when talking about work experience is not that you washed dishes; rather, what did you learn about working and about taking responsibility?"

Do not include salary information. It merely reflects your worth prior to the college education you now have to offer.

If you earned a significant percentage (50% or more) of your college expenses, consider mentioning that fact on your resume.

If you have done a lot of volunteer work that is appropriate to the career field in which you are interested, consider listing it under work experience rather than personal interests.

Personal Interests

You should have from three to eight items under this heading. One or more may be shared with your interviewer, resulting in more readily established rapport. Include varied interests to convey the fact that you're well rounded. An example or two of your intellectual, cultural, physical, and hobby interests will serve to do so.

Other Items

For each of the items on the following list, think through whether any of your involvements are deserving of an entry for one or more. Then, either show each as a separate section on your resume, or integrate into one of the sections above. The important point is not to omit any which might help project your desirability as a potential employee.

> Memberships (professional organizations, clubs, associations)
> Honors, awards (in addition to those education-related)
> Published works
> Job-related courses
> Certificates, licenses
> Special skills or assets
> Military experience
> Internships
> Languages

IN BRIEF

This chapter covered the background work necessary to design a resume. Now you must decide on an appropriate format, and bring the resume's various parts together to produce a successful product. How to do so is the subject of Chapter 6.

6

Resumes II: Successful Packaging

A successful salesperson recognizes that in today's consumer-oriented marketplace, competition is such that without the help of sales tools and techniques, even a superior product will often be ignored by the buying public. In the employment market, where there are sometimes hundreds of applicants for a single opening, your job will be to find the most effective tools to use in your sales campaign, then to develop techniques for their use that will result in a final "Sold." This chapter and the next will concentrate on the tools you will need, with techniques explored in later chapters.

Before a product reaches the marketplace, manufacturers spend considerable time, money, and effort in its packaging. They know that it is often the attractiveness of the package that makes one product move off store shelves more quickly than others. Before the product even can be examined by consumers, it must be chosen from an array of competitors. The same is true in the job market, where your resume serves as the packaging for the product you are selling. An extensive survey showed that two out of every three resumes —

a whopping 68 percent — are simply scanned for less than a minute. And a full 90 percent — nine out of ten — are read for two minutes or less!

Your first undertaking, then, is to come up with packaging for your training, skills, and abilities which will make those first thirty or sixty seconds count and lead to an interview in which your product may be fully examined. It is not stretching the truth to say that *no single tool is more important in your search for a job than your resume!*

It must be strong enough to be singled out for special attention, or you may never be called in for the interview that can lead to hiring. It also must be well thought out to serve as an outline for discussion so that the interview itself will follow an organized plan. Finally, it must be a complete, concise, and visually appealing document which will serve as a positive reminder of your application after the interview.

> The resume is probably the most important single selling tool. Don't let it be just a dull listing of school and other achievements to date. Find ways to make it stand out from the dozens of others. It should reflect your personality and talents.
>
> JAMES S. FISH
> RETIRED SENIOR VICE PRESIDENT
> GENERAL MILLS

RESUME FORMATS

How you put your resume together — its design or format — is almost as important as what you put in it. Consider each of the following basic formats to find the most effective packaging for your *You* product, always remembering that there is *no one right way*. You must tailor your own for the best fit.

The Chronological Resume

This type of resume is the best known to most applicants, and is by far the easiest to write. It consists of a simple listing of educational and work experience in chronological order, beginning with the most recent degree or job, working backward. One of its greatest advantages is that it provides screeners a quick, easy-to-read training and experience history in the form with which they are most familiar. And if your experience to date — both in school and in work — has been a steady progression upward, that record of consistent progress is put in the best perspective.

Perhaps the major disadvantage of the chronological resume is that it can be dull. Your experience is clearly set forth, of course, but there is little opportunity to focus attention on facets which may be the most meaningful in relation to the job for which you are applying (although you should be sure to state job-related accomplishments whenever possible).

It is human nature to attach importance to facts in the order in which they are presented. For instance, if a summer job two years ago has more bearing on the job you now want than last year's, and your performance was especially brilliant, some of the value of that experience is lost simply because the less important data comes first in your resume. Valued skills may not be spotlighted, since they are not reflected in your most recent job or schooling. Conversely, your last job or schooling assumes undue emphasis, even though it may be irrelevant to the position you are seeking.

Figure 6.1 shows a chronological resume which reflects a history with no actual work experience, while education and work experience both appear in chronological order in Figure 6.2. Most often, resumes are prepared flush to the left margin, but the centered form shown in Figure 6.2 has eye appeal and some distinctiveness, helping set it apart from many others.

Another example of a chronological resume appears in Figure 6.3. Note how Maria Mirto worked personal assets into her objective. And for each employer listed in her "Experience" section, she shows a "Primary Gain," which communicates effectively in the kinds of employment-related terms a resume reviewer is likely to think. Although her resume is basically a chronological format, Maria added several "Leadership Achievements" — the sort of entry typically found on a functional format (see below). The overall impression one gets from Maria's resume is that of a highly desirable candidate who has a good deal to offer and is serious about seeking a responsible position in her chosen field. Effective resumes like hers will stand out among the large numbers of typically sterile resumes through which employers must wade.

The Functional Resume

By organizing your resume to reflect your qualifications without regard to dates, you have much more latitude in stressing those skills most useful in the job for which you are applying. Professional growth can be highlighted even if it has been interrupted. Significant accomplishments can be listed up front to make use of the "first read" advantage. This type of resume is especially valuable if you

THOMAS A. SCOTT
123 Harding Road
Minneapolis, Minnesota 89101
(612) 123-4567

OBJECTIVE   Entry-level position, in advertising account management, requiring applicable education and highly developed interpersonal skills and leadership potential.

EDUCATION

B.S., Advertising and Telecommunications, DEF University, June 1981. Presently studying advertising media at School of Visual Arts, and conversational French at Language Communications Center.

REPRESENTATIVE ADVANCED COURSES

Principles of Advertising—Advertising history, purposes, techniques, media and research; analysis of the functions of advertising organizations.

Advertising Copywriting—Examination of advertising appeals, techniques, and their application to creative problems in copywriting.

Advertising Media Production—Survey of ad production for all media; introduction to visualization, layout, printing, cinematography, TV and radio production.

Advertising Campaigns—Analysis of the planning, financing and execution of campaigns through the case study method.

Broadcast Copywriting—Writing various types of radio and TV copy.

HONORS

Dean's List: 1978-79, 1979-80.

ON-CAMPUS MEMBERSHIPS

University Ad Club, President

XYZ Fraternity, Pledgemaster

Dolphin Swim Club

Hamsters Club

Footlight Theatre

EXTRACURRICULAR ACTIVITIES

University Yearbook, Business Manager, 1980

Organized student tour of principal French cities and provinces, 1979

Spring Weekend, Publicity Committee Co-chair, 1979

PERSONAL INTERESTS

Licensed ham radio operator

YMCA Youth Club volunteer (organized cultural programs)

Hi-fi recording

Swimming

Amateur theatre

FIGURE 6.1

THOMAS A. SCOTT
123 Harding Road
Minneapolis, Minnesota 89101
(612) 123-4567

OBJECTIVE

Entry-level position, in advertising account management, requiring applicable education and highly developed interpersonal skills and leadership potential.

EDUCATION

B.S., Advertising and Telecommunications, DEF University, June 1981. Presently studying advertising media at School of Visual Arts, and conversational French at Language Communications Center.

HONORS

Dean's List: 1978-79, 1979-80

WORK EXPERIENCE

(Summers and between school sessions)
Paid director of student tour to principal French cities and provinces, 1979 (Flair Tours, Inc.)

Devised sales campaign keyed to local events while employed in radio sales and copywriting, WFMZ-AM&FM: 20% increase in spot commercials. 1977-1979.

Designed window displays resulting in increased sales, while working as salesman, 1976. (Wolff's Men's Store)

ON-CAMPUS MEMBERSHIPS

University Ad Club (President); XYZ Fraternity (Pledgemaster); Dolphin Swim Club; Hamsters Club; Footlight Theatre.

EXTRACURRICULAR ACTIVITIES

Business Manager, University Yearbook, 1980; Organized student tour of principal French cities and provinces, 1979; Publicity Co-chair, Spring Weekend, 1979.

PERSONAL INTERESTS

Licensed ham radio operator; YMCA Youth Club volunteer (organized cultural programs); Hi-fi recording; Swimming; Amateur Theater.

FIGURE 6.2

MARIA C. MIRTO

244 Laurel Lane Clark, New Jersey 07066 (201) 381-7085

OBJECTIVE
Assistant Account Executive with an advertising agency — especially where a sense of responsibility, an ability to work with individuals and groups, and marketing, communication and creative skills are assets.

EDUCATION
NEW YORK UNIVERSITY New York, NY
Masters of Business Administration in February, 1981
Major: Marketing. . .Grade Point Average: 3.35. . .Member: American Marketing Association. . .Strongest subjects: Advertising Management, International Marketing Management, Legal/Social Context of Business

UNIVERSITY OF NOTRE DAME South Bend, IN
Bachelor of Arts in May, 1978. . .Major: Communication Arts/American Studies. . . Grade Point Average: 3.34. . .Honors: named to Dean's List for five semesters: chosen a Notre Dame Scholar. . .Strongest subjects: Telecommunications, Writing for Publication, Visual Communications

EXPERIENCE
EMPACADORA NACIONAL, S. A. Fairfield, NJ
Coordinated a study of the national marketing of frozen shrimp. . .supervised research program to evaluate consumer attitudes; developed package design for test marketing. . .(1979-80)

Primary Gain: introduction to the tasks of new product development. . .personal growth from working with those of varied international backgrounds

PERCEPTION RESEARCH SERVICES Englewood Cliffs, NJ
A market research analyst studying effectiveness of product advertisements and packaging. . .designed client surveys; interpreted research data; prepared final report. . .(Summer 1978)

Primary Gain: sparked interest towards a Marketing career. . .confidence in abilities to learn quickly and to inspire trust from co-workers

WNDU-TV (NBC affiliate) South Bend, IN
An intern in the Advertising/Promotions department. . .sold air time to local merchants; developed media strategies and budget plans for advertisers; supervised production of commercials. . .(1977-78)

Primary Gain: familiarity with the operation of a small television station. . . opportunity to put creative abilities to an effective use

LEADERSHIP
ACHIEVEMENTS
Elected Dormitory Vice-President. . .Wrote and produced documentary for local television. . .Advertising manager for publication of novel written by students. . .

Organized campus fund-raising contest that collected $1000 for local charity. . . Taught a seminar course for freshmen

PERSONAL
DATA
Born June 2, 1956. . .single. . .enjoys travel, sports, photography, music. . .considered a fast learner. . .works well under pressure. . .desires variety, creative challenges, excitement and competition

FIGURE 6.3

have a brief employment history or have held a number of widely differing jobs. Names of previous employers, with or without dates of employment, usually follow the functional listing.

Functional resumes can work especially well for those seeking entry-level positions because they give you the opportunity to focus on transferable skills — the aptitudes, talents, or experiences which you could apply to any number of positions. (In Figure 6.4, data from Figures 6.1 and 6.2 have been re-arranged in the functional format.) The key element, of course, is the section where you describe qualifications or skills. There is literally an endless number of possible entries on a functional resume. Your entries will come from your own work experiences and activities, highlighted by the worksheets and lists discussed later in this chapter. To help trigger your own thinking, Figure 6.5 is a listing of functional skills which other resume writers have found helpful in presenting themselves.

Holly A. Rosenthal, whose resume appears in Figure 6.6, very successfully combined the chronological and functional approaches. Although her work experience is presented in date order, she emphasizes the functional aspects involved in each of the positions she held. Note, too, the inclusion of achievements on the job, as well as her ability to project a positive image about each position (as opposed to a mere listing of duties, so typical of most resumes).

The Creative Resume

The creative resume is presented in a form "created" by the applicant. It may differ from the norm in content, arrangement, color or type of paper, graphics, or any combination of these factors. There are no rules for either its form or its appropriate use. Good judgment is the key here. If imagination is a requirement for the job you want, your creative resume can demonstrate that you have it. If the field you are entering places a high value on flair and style, this is your first opportunity to present your qualifications in an eye-catching, stylish manner.

Be forewarned, however, that in many fields outside communications, sales or the creative arts, employers may look on creative resumes with some degree of mistrust. Where conservative attitudes prevail, it is best to stick to a chronological or functional approach.

Figure 6.7 is a creative resume written by Karl G. Dentino, a candidate seeking a position in direct-mail advertising. It is an example of an innovative, well-executed, extremely attractive approach which is sure to result in a better-than-average number of interview invitations.

Bill Bergman's unusual, highly professional resume earned him

THOMAS A. SCOTT
123 Harding Road
Minneapolis, Minnesota 89101
(612) 123-4567

OBJECTIVE

Entry-level position, in advertising account management, requiring applicable education and highly developed interpersonal skills and leadership potential.

QUALIFICATIONS

Initiative

Radio sales and copywriter: Devised campaign for spot commercials, keyed to local events, which increased sales by 20% for local AM-FM station.

Business manager for University yearbook: Designed media plan, organized advertising solicitation program, sold yearbook advertising, instituted campus promotion campaign. All resulted in record yearbook sales.

Salesman: On own initiative, created appealing window displays for men's clothing store. Attracted measurably more new customers than previous displays.

Communication Skills

Able to communicate well orally and in writing—clearly, concisely and effectively.

Have developed interview skills as yearbook business manager.

Leadership and Managerial Skills

President of University Ad Club: Organized college poster service and directed club members in design, layout and printing of posters for 25 businesses catering to college market.

Director of student tour: Organized tour of major French cities and provinces. Set up itinerary, made all travel arrangements and accommodation bookings, coordinated sightseeing and free time activities for 20 university students.

YMCA Youth Club volunteer: Developed and directed cultural programs for 30 boys ages 12-16, including museum visits, concerts and literature readings.

Captain, University swim team: Organized intramural competitions and coordinated travel plans. Co-hosted visiting teams.

Human Relations Skills

Attentive listener, able to help people to "think out loud," reflect on experiences, identify problems, develop solutions.

Able to achieve warm rapport quickly and easily, putting others at ease.

Active commitments to community service and university organizations.

EMPLOYERS

WFMZ-AM&FM	1977-79
Flair Tours, Inc.	1979
Wolff's Men's Store	1976

EDUCATION

B.S., Advertising and Telecommunications, DEF University, June 1981.

Presently studying advertising media at School of Visual Arts, and conversational French at Language Communications Center.

INTERESTS

Ham radio (licensed operator); youth activities (YMCA Youth Club volunteer); hi-fi recording; swimming; amateur theater.

FIGURE 6.4

FUNCTION	EXAMPLES
Administering	Programs; people; clerical functions; budgets.
Analyzing	Qualitative, quantitative, statistical or scientific data; human relations situations; counseling.
Anticipating	Sensing what is likely to occur.
Budgeting	Money; time; resources.
Calculating	Mathematical, technical, time or space-related computations; assessing results/risks of activity.
Coaching	Athletics; academics.
Communicating	Orally; in writing; symbolically.
Controlling	People; finances; environmental conditions.
Coordinating	People; events; information; time sequences.
Counseling	Personal; educational; financial; technical.
Creating	Ideas; visual or performing arts; problem solving; inventions; writing.
Deciding	Alternate courses of action; use of resources.
Delegating	Assignments and responsibility to others.
Designing	Exteriors, interiors, contents; programs; approaches to problem solving or task execution.
Editing	Manuscripts; news matter; film.
Entertaining	Individuals; groups; audiences.
Estimating	Future income; physical space; probable costs or amounts.
Evaluating	Programs; services; individual or group performance.
Initiating	Ideas, methods, approaches; social contacts.
Interviewing	Judging applicants for qualification; obtaining information from people, organizations.
Managing	Getting things done through others; information or data; team or group activities; organization or program objectives.
Motivating	Convincing others to participate and perform.
Negotiating	Between individuals or groups; contracts.
Organizing	Coordinating individual efforts to accomplish group tasks; information, data.
Persuading	Points of view; getting others to react.
Planning	Events; programs; systems; needs; time schedules; itineraries.
Programming	Computers; events; systems.
Recording	Qualitative, quantitative, scientific or technical data; audio-visual.
Relating	Customers; work associates; social contacts; complaint or confrontation resolution.
Representing	School to potential students; employer to the public; products/services to users.
Researching	Background information; underlying causes of events or problems.
Selling	Products; services; ideas.
Supervising	Overseeing others; property; programs.
Teaching	Tutoring; classes; non-school groups.
Tolerating	Pressures from events, time, people; performance and views of others; lack of support for your own interests; misunderstandings.

FIGURE 6.5

```
┌─────────────────────────────────────────────────────────────────────────────────┐
│                                                                                   │
│  ─────────────────────       Box #1130, 3600 Chestnut St., Phila., Pa. 19104  (215) 349-8092  │
│  HOLLY A. ROSENTHAL  ─────────────────────────────────────────────────────────── │
│  ─────────────────────       311 Kneeland Ave., Yonkers, N.Y.  10705  (914) 965-1313          │
```

OBJECTIVE

A position in account and product management, consulting, or the marketing of services.

EDUCATION

The Wharton Graduate School of the University of Pennsylvania.
Master of Business Administration Degree Candidate, May, 1980.
   Concentration in Product Management, Advertising, and Market Research.
   Concurrent studies include Strategic Planning, Finance, and Quantitative Analysis.
   Record of High Achievement.

Consulted for the Hospital of the University of Pennsylvania. Active in the Marketing Association.

Cornell University College of Human Ecology.
Bachelor of Science Degree, May 1978.
   Management overview incorporating consumer economics, research design and analysis, accounting, motivational psychology, and business administration.
   Dean's List.

Appointed to the Cornell Council Committee, the Ambassadors, and served as an Orientation Counselor.

HONORS

- New York State Regents Scholarship
- National Merit Commendation
- Was commissioned to publish Resource Directory of Services for Tioga County, New York.

EXPERIENCE

Product Management　　　　　　　　　　　　　　　　SEPT. 1979—PRESENT, ATHLETICA, INC.

Partner in firm marketing new athletic product. Designed and implemented research for use in marketing strategy. Developed channels of distribution. Planned advertising campaign featuring ads in nationally circulated magazines. Was responsible for product line extensions and modifications.

Advertising and Sales Promotion　　　　　　　　　　　　SUMMER 1979, MACY'S NEW YORK

- Advertising Agency Project:
   Overviewed newspaper scheduling, layout, production of art and type, direct mail, broadcast, publicity, and special events. Aided in collecting, collating, and utilizing advertising statistics and assumed responsibilities within the business office.
- Marketing Management:
   Analyzed sales and stock history for recognition of emerging trends. Tested market for interpretation of customer wants to make effective buying decisions regarding product choice, pricing, and promotion. Aided in allocating resources to maintain maximum profitability, and in seasonal planning.

Operations Management　　　　　　　　　　　　　　　SUMMER 1978, HIT OR MISS STORES

Managed retail store with annual sales of over $1. million. Completed training program in three weeks and undertook full responsibility for marketing, and financial and inventory control. Trained and supervised management and sales personnel.

Organizational Initiation　　　　　　　　　　　　1978—1979, TIOGA OPPORTUNITIES PROGRAM

Created a service bringing together youngsters with selected adults for personal enrichment. Prepared and presented funding proposal before community executive board. Coordinated promotional campaign: Appeared on television, wrote copy for and scheduled broadcast and print advertisements.

Manufacturing　　　　　　　SUMMERS 1975, 1976, UNITED MERCHANTS AND MANUFACTURERS

Was selected for cross-functional program including projects in sales, information systems, and traffic departments.

PERSONAL

Energetic, creative, aesthetically oriented. Leadership abilities demonstrated in employment and the direction of numerous recreational and educational programs. Interests include Health Care, Writing, Water Sports, Antiques, and Woody Allen.

FIGURE 6.6

Attention Advertising Executives! When You're Ready To Make A Sound Investment . . .

Here Are Five Profitable Reasons Why You Should Hire This Adman

EXPERIENCE:
1. The main reason.

An adman is measured by his track record. Past performance is the best thing he can offer you. Hiring people without experience can be risky and costly. Karl Dentino comes to your firm with one year of part-time agency experience with Serpente, Wharton & Associates Advertising (May 1977 to May 1978). During that year he also worked with the Community Relations Department at Glassboro State College (September 1977 to May 1978).

Karl has previously worked for two retail establishments: Two Guys Department Store (1975-76), and Spencer Gifts (1974-75).

ADVERTISING SKILLS:
2. The tools.

Over the years, advertising has developed a body of research. Proven selling techniques have removed much costly guesswork. Facts, not opinions, make good ads. At Serpente, Wharton & Associates, Karl was taught the facts. He was trained in the direct response advertising philosophy. He learned the tested principles of direct response copywriting, and possesses the necessary ingredients for a career as an up and coming direct response copywriter.

Karl also developed and administered market surveys for a major supermarket account, compiled mailing lists for a direct mail account, and developed media estimates for industrial accounts.

In addition, Karl worked for two years as a retail salesperson for Two Guys Department Store and Spencer Gifts. This experience served as the baptismal ground for a career where persuasiveness, reliability, and the ability to communicate effectively are so vital.

Karl also holds a 3rd Class FCC Broadcasting License.

EDUCATION:
3. Laying the groundwork.

A sound academic background is no longer a luxury for prospective advertising people. Today it's a necessity. Karl Dentino has solid training in the study of advertising. He brings to your firm a B.A. in Communications from Glassboro State College (May 1978), with a concentration in advertising, and a minor in marketing. He graduated with cum laude honors, a 3.50 grade point average.

Direct Marketing Honors!

Karl Dentino was one of thirty-three advertising students from across the country awarded a scholarship to the Direct Mail/ Marketing Association (DMMA) Collegiate Institute. The week-long seminar, held in New York, covered all the principles of Direct Marketing and Direct Mail Advertising. This training gives Karl practical knowledge in an area not taught in most universities and colleges in the country.

LEADERSHIP QUALITIES:
4. How to recognize a leader.

A leader is a special breed of person. He accepts that extra responsibility which sets him apart from the others. You would know a leader -- because you are one. And, you will recognize this potential in Karl Dentino.

For three years Karl served as Vice-President of the Advertising Club at Glassboro State College. He helped club membership grow from five to twenty-five. He coordinated field trips to advertising agencies and arranged for advertising professionals to speak at club meetings.

Karl also served as Advertising Director for Student Activities Board Concerts (SAB) for two years. He was responsible for the promotion, logo design, and naming of an annual outdoor music festival held at Glassboro. The "Sunshine Jam" attracts more than 2500 students each year. He also wrote and designed ads for other SAB events.

SELF MOTIVATION:
5. The deciding factor.

Self motivation is the personality trait that separates the superior adman from the mediocre. Mediocre advertising people come a dime a dozen. And they usually don't last too long. The self motivator comes with full realization that hard work gets results. He knows his potential, and he knows how to reach it.

Karl Dentino has the self motivation you are looking for. He is ready to roll up his sleeves and get things done. He seeks a career with your firm, not just a job.

Karl is never satisfied with his present knowledge of advertising and he's always eager to learn more. That's why he is currently enrolled at Charles Morris Price School of Advertising and Journalism in Philadelphia (evening classes). And that's why he served for two years on the Advertising Staff of his college newspaper handling copywriting, layout, and paste-up.

ADVERTISING PHILOSOPHY:

Karl believes that all advertising should be based on a marketing plan. The plan, in turn, should be based on research of the product, its market, and its distribution. The over-all plan objective should be to increase the sale of the product. So advertising is actually selling.

If your advertising meets these selling standards, then Karl Dentino will meet your standards. For a free demonstration of Karl's selling abilities, fill out and mail the enclosed reply card. Or better yet, call Karl today at (609) 662-0387. He'll show you how to make a sound investment.

Do it today! This offer expires as soon as Karl gets a job.

WHAT OTHERS SAY ABOUT KARL DENTINO

"Articulate, enthusiastic, lots of potential." - Joseph Serpente, President, Serpente, Wharton & Associates, Mt. Laurel, New Jersey.

"Fine student, bright future in advertising." - Steven Le Shay, President, Le Shay Advertising LTD., Malaga, New Jersey.

"Firm grasp on the direct response copy principles." - Frank Grazian, Associate Prof. of Communications, Glassboro State College, Glassboro, New Jersey.

KARL G. DENTINO
3330 Hollywood Circle
Pennsauken, New Jersey 08109
(609) 662-0387

6'1"
175 lbs.
September 19, 1956
Single

FIGURE 6.7

When you're 21 and fresh out of college you gotta be willing to work your tail off to be good.

Whiz kids aren't born overnight. It's 28-hour days, sleepless nights and a real love for advertising that has made them successful.

Sure. It's easy to say that you like advertising. But to sincerely love the business you've got to enjoy the tension, the pressure and the millions of headaches that accompany fierce competition.

My name is Bill Bergman and this May I'll be graduating from the University of Oklahoma with a degree in advertising and marketing.

In four years of college I didn't achieve academic success through luck. It was hard work and a real love for what I was studying that has allowed me to maintain a 3.6 overall grade average.

Grades alone though are only an indicator of one's ability. So let me tell you a little bit more about what I've done in the past four years.

Work Experience

I've had quite a bit of experience in journalism and advertising in school as well as in the summers.

For two summers now I've worked at Peter Mayer Advertising in New Orleans, my hometown.

The first summer I was an office boy.

The next summer, though, I worked in the account services department doing marketing research for the agency's biggest client, Wembley Ties. Also, I assisted account executives on many of the agency's retail accounts.

Here at school I've been business manager of the yearbook. Managing editor of the *Forum* which is a national publication of the Public Relations Student Society of America. And I've been a staff writer, wire editor and most recently a columnist on the campus newspaper, the *Oklahoma Daily*.

Finally, last year I was a counselor in the dorms planning activities and helping 62 residents cope with the problems of college life.

Major Campus Activities

As president of the Stewart Harrell chapter of the Public Relations Student Society of America, I have helped in bringing speakers to campus as well as organizing promotional campaigns for student organizations.

As a member of the debate team, I've participated in intercollegiate debate tournaments on such topics as national health care.

When I was pledge trainer of the Alpha Epsilon Pi social fraternity, I spent many sleepless nights helping freshmen face the problems of adjusting to a new way of life.

In an advertising campaigns class, I served as president and creative director of a student ad agency that was in competition with three other agencies all pitching for the same account. My agency won by a unanimous vote of the journalism and marketing faculty, and a group of advertising professionals.

And as a member of the University of Oklahoma Speakers Forum, I was a major speaker on the topic of Women's Liberation.

References

Selling myself, my ideas and my organizations is what has made my college years so successful.

Guiding and teaching me through these years have been three people. They are:

Peter A. Mayer, President
Peter Mayer Advertising, Inc.
816 Howard Ave.
New Orleans, Louisiana 70113

Nora Owens, Vice President
Lowe Runkle Company
1800 Liberty Tower
Oklahoma City, Oklahoma 73102

Frank Heaston
Professor of Advertising
(15 years with Gardner Advertising)
Copeland Hall
860 Van Fleet Oval
Norman, Oklahoma 73069

Why hire Bill Bergman?

Youth. Aggressiveness. And a strong desire to learn is what I have to offer.

I'll work my tail off because it's hard work and a sincere love for what you're doing that makes advertising such an exciting business.

If you're interested and you'd like to meet me, write me at my school address:

1705 E. Lindsey
Apt. 2
Norman, Oklahoma 73069
(405) 329-1519

or at my permanent home address:

2114 Jefferson Ave.
New Orleans, Louisiana 70115
(504) 891-6531

FIGURE 6.8

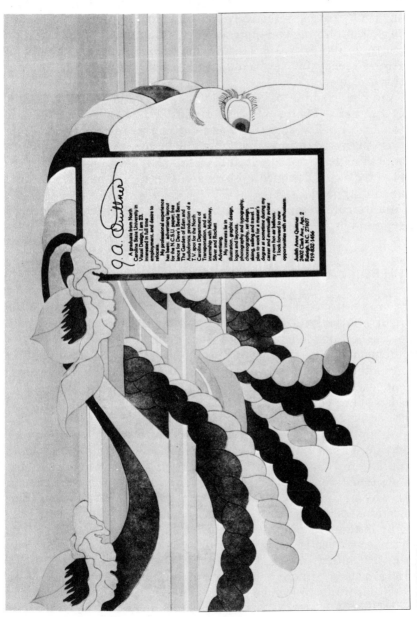

FIGURE 6.9

a large number of interviews (see Figure 6.8). His goal is clear: he wants advertising and so he writes an ad selling himself. He uses first person ("I," "me") effectively, maintaining a proper degree of humility. His photo, while unorthodox, is inviting. (Bill decided he wanted to go on for an MBA degree and then look for a spot with an advertising agency in New York. The resume he designed for that effort is in Appendix C.)

Another example of an outstanding creative resume is Judith Anne Quittner's, Figure 6.9. The original was a four-color production on high quality stock. It was so attractive that more than one reviewer suggested it was "suitable for framing." Black-and-white reproduction does not do it full justice, but its uniqueness is apparent. (Judy also designed a black and white "self-mailer" resume, included in Appendix C.)

Additional examples of creative, innovative resume approaches can be found in Appendix C.

WHICH FORMAT IS RIGHT FOR YOU?

There are no ironclad rules for determining which resume format is the right one for you. You are the only one who can judge which makes the best possible presentation for your *You* product.

Remember, the resume will nearly always be your introduction to any potential employer; it will make that crucial first impression. Eye appeal, clarity, readability, and some degree of personality should be your goals when writing a resume. It is for you to decide which format best accomplishes these goals.

An option far too few people recognize is the possibility of having more than one resume. If a functional resume seems most appropriate for one group of employers, while a creative format best suits another (even though both target groups are in the same general field), why not prepare both? For example, if you have chosen communications as your career, the public relations department of a bank or insurance company may offer an attractive starting point. Such an employer is going to be interested in applicants who can turn out dignified, trust-inspiring copy. On the other hand, an advertising agency which handles commercial accounts is likely to respond positively to evidence of imagination, wit, and eye-catching flair. In your job search, both possibilities may well be of interest to you, yet each calls for a different resume approach and possibly a slight difference in your job objective statement. By preparing a functional or chronological resume for institutional applications and a creative resume for agencies, you will be ready to apply for openings in either. It involves an extra effort, but it can pay big dividends.

An equally important reason for having more than one resume would be your interest in several different types of entry-level positions. It is entirely possible that one person qualifies for, and is interested in, these jobs: Financial Analysis & Planning; Brand Management; Marketing Research; Consulting Services. If the candidate lists all four on a resume, there is a risk that some (perhaps many) screeners would reject the applicant with the rationale: "This candidate doesn't know what he wants to do." You can avoid this potential trap by having a separate resume for each distinct field of job interest you have. Very closely related goals, of course, can appear on the same resume.

REVISIONS

The first draft of your resume should be viewed only as a starting point. Go over it again and again to spot verbs that can be strengthened, phrases or sentences that can be shortened to add punch, and any omissions that weaken it. Double check grammar, spelling, and punctuation. Rewrite until you are satisfied it is accurate, complete, truthful, and *positive.* Then, test your draft on others you can rely on to give you an objective and honest opinion. Show it to someone who doesn't know you well and allow 30-60 seconds reading time, then ask for a description of your background based on that reading. (That's the time range professional recruiters will usually give it.) If your *You* product is fuzzy in the reader's mind after the scanning, go back to the drawing board to revise and revise and revise until a clear, sharp image comes across at first glance. Ernest Hemingway was once asked why he had rewritten a particular paragraph eight times. His answer: "To get the right words."

This advice from S. Watson Dunn, dean of the University of Missouri's College of Business and Public Administration, applies generally to the entire job-seeking process, but is especially pertinent when considering the effort necessary to produce an effective resume: "If young job seekers take a careful, well-planned, professional approach in marketing their own services, the chances are good that the would-be employer would assume that they would be just as careful and professional in the marketing of whatever goods or services that company is trying to promote."

YOUR RESUME'S FINAL LOOK

By now, you have a substantial investment of time and effort in putting together your resume. Yet all that can be for naught if it arrives on the recruiter's desk without eye appeal. The most effective qualifications, presented in the most appropriate format, lose import when presented via a smudgy carbon of a typed original. Even on a typed original a faint typewriter ribbon or dirty keys will convey a negative impression. Mechanics are especially important in the production of your resume. The quality of graphics and materials are equal in importance to content.

Remember, your resume is a projection of *you*. It must make an instant positive impression. This is not the place to skimp on expense. Spend what you must to have the final product do you proud — it is a monetary investment in yourself that will make the others pay off.

Basically, these are the mechanics which will make the difference:

- Use standard business-letter sized paper (8½″ x 11″). Odd sized documents cause filing problems in most offices.
- Avoid a cluttered look. Leave space between sections. An effective resume, like an effective advertisement, makes good use of white space to "frame" the content.
- If at all possible, have your resume typeset and printed. The cost is nominal, the difference phenomenal! A good place to begin your price survey is the printer who handles your school publications. Be sure a good (not extravagant) quality paper will be used. And insist on proofreading the copy yourself before the final printing — the screener will not know if an error is the typesetter's or yours.
- If your resume is typed, be sure the machine has a new ribbon, keys are clean, and the typeface is businesslike (no script or other hard-to-read typeface). Also, stick to offset or letterpress printing or a similar quality duplicating process, *not* copy machines, mimeograph, spirit duplicators, or the like.
- If you have decided on a creative resume, be sure your graphics are of top quality. Consider having a professional illustrator design them, keeping in mind that they must reproduce cleanly and clearly, with no fuzzy edges. Remember, too, that resumes of any format must be filed in standard size cabinets, so keep your "creative size" reasonable enough to wind up in permanent files designed for 8½″ x 11″ materials, not the wastebasket.

74

Employee relations people, when planning programs for their companies, often given attention to how effective such programs will be in attracting, retaining, and motivating staff. That's because they know that by doing so, their chances for heightened receptivity of their efforts will be increased.

You can, and should, take a similar approach — with a variation. As you prepare your resume, cover letter, and other written communications, keep the elements of *attention, persuasion,* and *motivation* in mind, because that is what you are out to do: attract the reader's attention, persuade the reader that you are a viable candidate, and motivate the reader to respond by inviting you for an interview.

ATTENTION
PERSUASION
MOTIVATION

are your criteria for effective resumes and other written communications. Apply them as a test for determining the effectiveness of every piece of job-related material you write.

IN BRIEF

In two of the most important chapters in this book, you have read about the importance of your resume; how to put together an effective resume; the different types of resumes; and the appearance of a resume which "sells" you. Now let's talk about an essential companion piece, your cover letter, as well as other written communications.

7

Effective
Cover Letters
and Other
Written Materials

The letter which transmits your resume to employers does many things. It is, in a very real sense, an advertisement for the *You* product you have to market.

The first requirement of an effective advertisement is that it have *appeal*. So, while the resume must be a concise, hard-hitting summary of all you have to offer, its cover letter is your chance to shine as a human being, and to demonstrate personal charm. It can highlight an accomplishment only mentioned briefly in your resume, or let the employer know you are willing to relocate, or name-drop if you have been referred by a mutual acquaintance.

Even more important, the cover letter can show the employer that you have, indeed, done your homework about the organization and make it clear that there are good and sufficient reasons to believe you can be an asset to it (all, of course, detailed in your attached resume).

Finally, the cover letter will ask for action from the employer, specifically, an interview in the immediate future. It will set out when and where you will be available for that interview.

In short, the cover letter adds to and reinforces your resume, just as that resume must add to and reinforce what is said in the letter, itself.

> If job seekers realized how important good written communications are, they would work much harder on the letters they write. Letters which accompany resumes are very often the only chance candidates have to convince employers to invite them in for interviews. Yet most of those letters are routine and uninspired. They don't motivate employers. They fail to project good reasons why their authors should be seen.
>
> LOUIS T. HAGOPIAN
> CHAIRMAN AND CHIEF EXECUTIVE OFFICER
> N W AYER INCORPORATED

PUTTING TOGETHER
A COVER LETTER

As with your resume, simple mechanics will help you put together an effective cover letter.

Style
Every cover letter should be written by you personally. Only if it is a proper reflection of your own personality will it serve as the reinforcement and advertisement you want for your resume.

Keep it businesslike, but with warm human touches. Examine each sentence to see if it is free of gimmickry and not stifled by clichés or triteness. This letter has a very serious purpose, and its tone should indicate that you are serious in your application. At the same time, if the letter is dull, you will be perceived as dull, and dullness does not sell!

Figure 7.1 shows a cover letter which strikes the right balance. A somewhat different approach to a cover letter, which worked well for its author, is shown in Figure 7.2.

Individually type each and every letter you send. You can not appeal specifically to potential employers with a pre-printed letter, not to mention the fact that it turns off most resume readers. If you care enough to apply to the organization, and expect individual attention and a response, extend your readers the courtesy of an individually typed letter (and be sure it is free of typographical, spelling, and grammatical errors, or noticeable erasures).

```
                                      123 Harding Road
                                      Minneapolis, MN  89101

                                      February 13, 1981



Mr. Charles W. Cleveland, President
Cleveland Advertising, Inc.
411 West Main Street
St. Paul, MN  90102

Dear Mr. Cleveland:

     Our mutual friend, George Gold, has suggested that I
write to you about possible employment, given my interest and
training in virtually all forms of advertising.

     In June of this year, I'll receive a B.S. in advertising
and telecommunications from DEF University, where I made Dean's
list for two consecutive years.  Studies in television and
cinematography supplement my experience and instruction in
radio copywriting and retail displays.

     My college education was largely financed through summer
employment, which has also enabled me to put classroom theory
into actual practice.  For example, during three summers with
radio station WFMZ-AM&FM, I devised and implemented a spot
commercial campaign tie-in with local sports and cultural
events, resulting in a 20% sales increase over the previous
year.

     In the visual arts area, I have experience in the design,
layout and production of posters in connection with a unique and
highly successful service for college-related businesses, organ-
ized while I was president of the University Ad Club.

     Because of your agency's outstanding reputation for creative,
successful advertising, I'm eager to discuss an entry position to
which I could make worthwhile contributions.  I'll take the liberty
of calling you Wednesday of next week, with the hope we can set a
meeting date.  Should you want to contact me in the meantime, I
can be reached at (612) 123-4567.

     I very much look forward to meeting you personally.

                                      Sincerely.



                                      Thomas A. Scott

cc: Mr. George Gold
```

FIGURE 7.1

```
                                        9 Tulip Terrace
                                        San Francisco, CA  94112
                                        April 17, 1981


   Mr. Steven R. Michaels
   Vice President, Client Services
   Rockford, Rose & Hollander
   1345 The Fairway
   Sacramento, CA  95834

   Dear Mr. Michaels:

        The other day I called on the General Manager of a large
   public accounting firm.  I briefed him on my successes at
   school, my broad-based experience as a result of several full
   and part-time jobs, and my reputation for accurate, timely
   work.  I know by the end of our discussion I had convinced
   him that I would make a strong new addition to his staff.

        "Jane," he said, "I really wish you had come by earlier
   because I just filled an opening for a new junior accountant
   last week."

        The purpose of this letter is to make your acquaintance
   before it's too late!

        My resume is enclosed.  I'll be happy to provide further
   details and show you examples of my work.

        Let's meet soon.  So we can set a date, I'll call you on
   the 27th.  If you'd like to reach me before then, my phone
   number is (415) 122-3344.

        I very much look forward to our personal meeting.

                                        Sincerely,



                                        Jane deLand Oliver

   cc: Ms. Mary Marks
       Personnel Manager
```

FIGURE 7.2

The *attention, persuasion, motivation* criteria discussed at the end of the previous chapter has as much application to cover letters as it does to resumes.

In considering your cover letter's style, keep in mind the golden rule of all successful writers: the reader's attention must be engaged at the outset. Make your opening sentence or paragraph a "grabber."

If you have been referred by someone known to the employer, say so at the beginning. Let it be known early on that you have the backing of someone the firm knows and respects.

If you are answering an ad, address the traits or qualifications mentioned as requirements. Use some of the same words in the ad; the employer has carefully chosen them as the most descriptive of the job, and strength is automatically added to your reply when you identify at the start with the qualities for which the employer is looking.

Or construct an interesting, arresting opening, likely to have appeal to the reader, in which you show your interest in working for the recipient's organization, or what you can bring to the organization if employed. Here are examples, from actual letters, which applied the principle of attracting attention at the start:

> Excuse me for writing to the top man, but since that's where I plan to be some day, I want him to know about me and, if he is willing, see me for employment.

> I'm ready! Equipped with my master's degree in international management, a bachelor's in accounting, and a lot of enthusiasm. I'm ready to start a career in finance with a worldwide company like International Technology.

> Good sales people are hard to find!
> I'm talking about the dynamic, aggressive, shirt-sleeves type who is willing to get the job done at all costs. A person who wants to learn, grow and be successful, and is not satisfied with 'satisfactory.'
> A marketing person who digs deep to the root of problems and then not only formulates solutions, but believes in active follow-through as well.

> I'm the product of a three-generation commitment to engineering: my father through aerospace; my grandfather through automotive.
> Now it's my turn.
> Just graduating from college, I'm eager to get my career rolling with a company like National Ceramics.

> Challenge and opportunity. Intangible though they are, their magnetism has drawn me from Boise to New York, the publishing industry's 'Wharton School of Experience'.

The Detroit Ledger is a name that means Journalism. And Journalism is where my ambitions lie. I am a senior at the University of Missouri School of Journalism, most interested in working for a quality paper like yours, in a major metropolitan area like Detroit.

What makes me different than all the other college graduates looking for entry-level opportunity at your bank? A successful record of diversified experience, an eager desire to learn, and the willingness and determination to get a job done. Those are the assets I offer you.

And finally, some advice from Thomas S. Carroll, president, Lever Brothers Company: "Try to develop an attention-getting approach to go with your letter and resume. For example, you might say you are willing to work as an intern for three months without any pay because of your admiration and faith in the company. Since they don't know you, you want to give them three months to find out how great you are. The point is that no company would accept this offer, but it certainly will attract the attention of the people to whom you are writing."

If you are sending an unsolicited application, be sure your cover letter shows an understanding of the organization's products or services. Demonstrate that you know what its needs are, and why you believe you can meet them in some way. One word of caution, however: avoid at all costs wording that sounds phony or overly complimentary. A gushy opening will do nothing but speed your letter and its accompanying resume to the rejection pile.

Reinforce your understanding of the organization's needs by listing concrete examples of traits, education, interests, or — strongest of all — accomplishments which fit those needs. Make this the very heart of your letter, and keep your statements short and crisp.

Close your letter by requesting an interview and letting the employer know when you will be available. Remember: you want to motivate your reader, and motivation means *move to action.* Most letter writers ask that the recipient contact them. That works sometimes, but not nearly as often as you would hope for. What is more likely to work is action which *you* take, such as closing your letter with: "Mr. Jones, I'll be in Chicago from December 16th through January 24th. Because I'm truly anxious to meet with you or someone on your staff, I'll call your office December 12th with the hope we can set a date."

Consider borrowing an idea from successful direct mail writers: use a "P.S." (which achieves high readership and response). For example:

P.S. Jack Smith, one of the new men in your Investigations Division, is a friend and classmate. Feel free to ask him about the contributions I could make to your company.

or,

P.S. I'll be in Omaha most of next week, getting my award from the Marketing Association's Educational Foundation. That may make me hard to reach, so I'll take the liberty of calling you on the 28th.

Keep your letter short—one page is likely to be read; two will probably be scanned.* Read your cover letter and ask yourself this question: Would you be persuaded to meet you? If the answer is "No," or "I'm not sure," *rewrite.* Keep doing this until you are satisfied your letter has a high likelihood of both attracting attention and persuading the reader to meet you. Then try it out on several others. If most agree, you can move ahead with greater assurance that your letter will spark the level of interest necessary to earn you a positive response.

Item by Item

To Whom Addressed. When possible, your cover letter and resume should be addressed directly to the person most likely to make the hiring decision (see Chapter 4). When in doubt, address it to a high-level executive in your functional area of interest; *never* use "To Whom It May Concern."

Be sure all names and positions are accurate and properly spelled. If the sources referred to in Chapter 4 fail to give you up-to-the minute information, a phone call to the organization's personnel or public relations department will get you spellings and current job titles.

Salutation. Always address the recipient by name: "Dear Mr. Jones," not "Dear Sir/Madam," or "Gentlemen."

Opening. Compose an opening sentence or paragraph which will immediately set your letter apart from others. Keep it as short as possible for the greatest effect, and avoid irrelevant or insincere wording.

Body. Make a careful study of your resume and select those facets of your education or work experience or personal interests which

*Two excellent resources for improving your written communications are: Say What You Mean, by Rudolph Flesch, Harper & Row; and On Writing Well, by William Zinsser, Harper & Row.

best fit this particular situation, then write short, punchy sentences to highlight the most significant. Do not simply repeat the information on your resume; emphasize or expand on it. Limit your examples to two or three which will have the greatest impact. Your resume contains less important qualifications as well, so use this letter to capitalize on your most effective selling points. A series of one-sentence paragraphs, each pointing out one reason you meet the employer's requirements, have far greater impact than long, autobiographical prose.

Close. Keep it brief, but be sure you explain how you will make contact, or request a reply. Tailor your request to the employer's convenience if you can.

THE APPEARANCE
OF YOUR COVER LETTER

As explained earlier, your cover letter should be a typed original and follow standard business form.

If you have a personal letterhead, use it. If not, use plain white or ivory (or some other neutral) color stationery, never anything flashy. Its size may vary from the standard 8½" x 11", but should not be larger, and it should be no smaller than monarch-size (6½" x 9"), as dimensions that vary too greatly take on the appearance of a gimmick and are hard to file.

As was cautioned in respect to the resume, be certain your typewriter has a legible ribbon and clean keys; that grammar, spelling, and punctuation are letter-perfect; and that your name, return address, and telephone number are shown prominently in the letter. Moreover, placement on the page should be such that the content is generously framed by white space.

OTHER WRITTEN COMMUNICATIONS

While cover letters are the most frequently used types of written communications, and for many job-seekers the only type of letter writing they do, there are times when other types of letters are necessary (or make sense, even if not required).

Although content and purpose may vary, principles are the same as for cover letters. In each you want to attract attention at the outset, persuade about one or more points in the body, and close with some type of attempt at motivating (or expressing appreciation to) your reader.

Figures 7.3 through 7.8 are examples of letters used for purposes other than accompanying resumes.

Figure 7.3 is a follow-up from a student who had not received a response to an initial mailing. Figure 7.4 is a response from a writer who had been rejected by mail, after forwarding his resume. Figure 7.5 is addressed to an on-campus recruiter in advance of his visit to the letter writer's school. Figure 7.6 follows word of rejection after an interview.

Figure 7.7 thanks an individual interviewer and Figure 7.8 does the same where a group interview was involved.

AVOID FREQUENTLY MADE ERRORS

Analysis of thousands of letters sent by job-seekers reveals ten errors found far too often. Any one of them might sufficiently irk your reader, causing you to be eliminated from consideration, or at the least, to raise questions about your potential professionalism. Study the following list carefully, and be sure none of your written communications include any of these:

1. Using pre-printed form letters rather than individually typed letters.
2. One or more spelling errors, typographical errors, or grammatical mistakes.
3. Using overly formal language, rather than writing as if having a conversation with the reader.
4. Typing on "eraseable" paper, resulting in smudges when handled.
5. Lack of organization. Failing to have an attention-getting opening, a persuasive middle section, and/or a motivating end.
6. Double-spacing letter so that it takes two pages to cover what could be said in one.
7. Lacking graphic appeal. Typed too high on page, margins too narrow, unclean typewriter keys, sloppy erasures, and so forth.
8. Paragraphs too long. Uninviting to reader.
9. Forgetting to sign letter, indicating lack of attention to detail.
10. Using one or more initials rather than first name, projecting coldness and leaving reader ignorant of whether a response should go to a "Mr." or a "Ms."

```
                                        290 Tennessee
                                        Lawrence, Kansas   66044
                                        January 6, 1981


        Mr. Cranston Poole
        Director of Personnel
        Social Welfare Department
        City of Minneapolis
        Minneapolis, Minnesota   55440

        Dear Mr. Poole:

             On December 15th I wrote to express my interest
        in possible employment with your agency.

             I have not yet had a response and it occurs to
        me that perhaps my first letter did not reach you.
        So I'm taking the liberty of sending you a copy of my
        earlier letter, together with my resume.

             I'll be in Minneapolis March 11th through 14th.
        Would you please take a moment to review the enclosed
        and let me know if you could schedule an interview
        with me during that period?

             I very much look forward to your positive reply.

                                        Sincerely yours,


                                        Lisa Telling
```

FIGURE 7.3

Hamilton Park
Wilshire Drive, Apt. 22E
Guilderland, New York   12084

January 18, 1981

Ms. Katherine Potts
Personnel Manager
Krona Rubber Company
Akron, OH   44309

Dear Ms. Potts:

   Your thoughtful letter of January 14 was most considerate,
although disappointing. While I was sorry to learn there are
no current openings for Krona's Supervisory Training Program,
I am asking you to keep my resume active for any future
possibilities.

   I believe a face-to-face meeting would be mutually beneficial.
I would have the opportunity to personally convey the strength
of my academic training, personal motivation and leadership
skills; you would have the chance to decide whether I would be
a likely candidate for future openings.

   Your company's reputation for excellence is predicated on
the work of talented professionals. You demand the exceptional.
I'd like to prove to you how valuable an addition to Krona I
would be.

   My genuine thanks for your courtesy and consideration.
I hope you agree that a personal meeting would be to mutual
advantage.

                        Sincerely,

                        Keith L. Fong

FIGURE 7.4

```
                    12 Richmond Road
                    Galveston, TX  77553
                    November 9, 1980



Mr. Harry T. White
General Manager
The Fun Farm, Inc.
Anaheim, California  92803

Dear Mr. White:

I was delighted to learn that your company will be
recruiting at the business school, here at Texas College.
As one of the few December graduates, I'm immediately
available for employment following graduation.

I have a strong operations/management background, enhanced
by extensive adtivities with the school's Marketing Club
and the local chapter of the American Management Association.

I'm enclosing my resume for your perusal prior to your
visit, and very much look forward to our personal meeting
on the 21st of this month (I'm the first person on your
schedule that morning).

My talents, background and interests are well-suited to
your posted openings.  I'm excited over the prospect of
working for The Fun Farm.  I'll try to prove that to you
when we meet!

With anticipation,


Richard P. C. Westminster

     (
```

FIGURE 7.5

April 14, 1981

Mrs. Ruth T. Bruce
V.P., Computer Services
Cambridge Manufacturing Company, Inc.
Orlando, Florida 32802

Dear Mrs. Bruce:

    I'd like to thank you once again -- this time for my interview with Bill Caney and conversations with Bella Carton about a place in Cambridge's management training program.

    I must admit that I was disappointed not to have been selected for it. I'm smart, educated, enthusiastic...with some relevant computer experience and a start on an MBA to add to my bachelor's in computer science.

    All this gives me the confidence that you might reconsider my candidacy, and hopefully make a place for me at Cambridge. Your company is the best in its field -- I'd very much like to be a part of your dynamic growth and supremacy.

    My visits gave me the chance to see how busy you are. In the interests of your time, I'll call you Tuesday morning, next week, for a quick "yes" or "no." I certainly hope it's the former!

                    Cordially,

                    Tony Lacki
                    12 Beachview
                    Jacksonville, Florida 32201

FIGURE 7.6

14 East 90th Street
Apartment 123
New York, N. Y. 10012
March 30, 1981

Mr. Marshall Rosenstein
Deputy Chairman, Planning Commission
The City of New York
City Hall
New York, N.Y.   10002

Dear Mr. Rosenstein:

   Thank you for a most informative, helpful and
enjoyable interview. After our conversation on
Tuesday I am more convinced than ever that my
decision to pursue a career in city planning is a
wise one.

   As we discussed, my background with the City of
Cleveland, while pursuing my college degree, gave me
a unique experience and exposure to both the operations and administrative aspects of planning. Along
with the interpersonal skills I've developed, and my
seriousness of purpose, my experience rounds out my
preparation to start my career in your exciting and
satisfying field.

   I anxiously look forward to hearing from you
regarding the next phase of the interviewing process.
Should you not be able to reach me at my home number,
feel free to leave a message with my father, John
Cappiola, at 992-3131.

                          Sincerely,

                          Mary Cappiola

FIGURE 7.7

One Hunt Lane
San Acacia, New Mexico 87831
April 3, 1981

Dolores vanSanto, Ph.D.
Superintendent of Schools
Greater Albuquerque School District #2
98 Taos Avenue
Albuquerque, New Mexico 87125

Dear Dr. vanSanto:

Many thanks for your coordination of my enjoyable and enlightening day last Thursday, March 29th. After interviewing with you and David Butt, Byron Caron, Gail Peterson and Alvera Vadito, the prospect of working for your progressive school district as a junior career counselor became a major priority towards the fulfillment of my career goals.

This letter comes to thank all of you for the time you spent with me, and the interest shown in my candidacy.

As I mentioned, my master's in counseling and my volunteer experience with San Acacia's "Project Job-Seek," would prove to be most helpful to your district's efforts. In addition, my demonstrated leadership qualities and analytical and organizational skills would be an asset to your extensive counseling efforts.

I look forward to hearing from you again soon and to beginning a rewarding career with the district.

Sincerely,

Geraldine Wyckoff

cc: Mr. David Butt
    Mr. Byron Caron
    Dr. Gail Peterson
    Ms. Alvera Vadito

FIGURE 7.8

IN BRIEF

This chapter highlighted the importance of the cover letter; how to write an effective one; the final appearance of your cover letter; advice on other written communications; and avoiding mistakes frequently made. Now that you have a handle on written materials needed for job finding, let us turn attention to the interviewing process.

8

Planning for Your Interviews

Here it is at last: interview time. The nitty-gritty of job hunting. The face-to-face confrontation that will bring together everything you have learned so far and determine how and where you will use it to make your living. It's scary, to say the least. Palms turn clammy. There's a knot in the pit of your stomach at the very thought. The mind that has converted sharp, clear facts into a terrific resume and a dynamite cover letter in the privacy of your own environment turns to mush when it contemplates discussing those same facts with an all-powerful interviewer on his or her turf.

Well, let's see if some of the fright can be taken out of interviews. First of all, we must admit up front that they *are* scary. After all, you *do* have a lot riding on them. They are among the most important conversations you will have in your entire life. But, on their most basic level, that is exactly what they are: conversations. Maybe you have never been interviewed for a job before, but you *have* had conversations since you first began to talk. Social conversations. Conversations to elicit information. Classroom conversations with professors and classmates. Conversations that turned into debates as you tried to convert someone to your way of thinking. Exploratory conversations to find out about a new acquaintance, to discover mutual interests and fundamental differences.

A close look at any interview will reveal elements of all those past conversations. So, in a sense, you have been acquiring interview skills unconsciously for a long time. The trick is to marshal them now to work for you. It's not as hard as you might think. No technique, of course, is going to remove all the tension from a job interview. But there are several that will make you more comfortable and more effective. It is not so much a matter of learning them as it is of recognizing them.

The interview, essentially, is a conversation to help both you and a prospective employer learn as much as possible about each other. The final "You're hired," or "Sorry, you're not quite what we're looking for" may be determined to a very large degree by what the interviewer finds out about you in this conversation. Equally important, your "I really want this job" or "It's not what I had in mind" will almost certainly be based on the things you learn about the company. Let's look, then, at just how you and your interviewer will go about reaching one of those conclusions.

WHAT THE INTERVIEWER WILL WANT TO KNOW

Basically, any employer considering your application is going to be looking for the following: *What* you are (your skills, abilities, basic knowledge); *who* you are (your personality, character, non-work interests); and *why* you should be hired, or why not. The interviewer will try to determine whether you, as a composite of all these attributes, will be an asset to the organization's operation.

You have, at this point, already done a pretty good job of setting forth the *what* in your resume, so that the company has at least a suspicion that you have what it needs in the way of background preparation. The interview will provide a setting to explore your skills, abilities, and general knowledge in more depth. It's all well and good to look at a record of college courses passed with high marks, but the employer will want to know how much of the content of those courses you've retained outside the classroom. In other words, if your education "took" — if you will be bringing to its payroll a solid foundation for the training it can give you.

Your interviewer will review the most important points in your resume, and you are in trouble if those points are not engraved on your mind! *Memorize your resume.* Know intimately, too, each selling point you so painstakingly developed for the cover letter. Know your own background forward and backward, and be ready to talk about it easily and naturally.

Beyond what you have been able to tell the organization on paper, your interviewer will want to get down to specifics, details not covered in your resume. This is where you can either shine or be counted out. If you are asked questions about a procedure that is outside your classroom study, you'll make points with a reply like "That's a very interesting application of the XYZ theory, and I'd like to know more about it." If the question raises a field of study foreign to your college curriculum, a wise reply is "That sounds like a fascinating field, and I certainly plan to look into it, as my college studies didn't cover it." In short, your strategy in this portion of the interview is to show that you have a grasp of the fundamentals of your field, and an interest in all its aspects. It is that interest that can turn a weakness into an asset.

On the other hand, nothing can be as deadly as trying to bluff when it comes to technical language. One use of the wrong term in the wrong context can betray you, and repeated wrong usage will confirm your subterfuge. That does not mean you must confess weakness because you are lacking in some area. It simply means you can acknowledge a deficiency, but stress your eagerness to learn. If you can illustrate that eagerness by referring to any kind of special classroom project (regardless of whether it relates to the topic at hand) that went beyond required study, so much the better. The interviewer then has hard evidence that you do, indeed, act on your professed interests.

Sometimes applicants have one or more things they hope will not be asked. Examples include poor grades, lack of extracurricular activities, being fired from a job for poor performance, unclear motivation for the career field in which they are applying, breaks in schooling, and so forth. If you are in that position, be sure you plan exactly how you will respond to such "sore point" questions. Better to be ready with a carefully prepared answer, than to stumble your way through during an interview.

THE "WHO" QUESTIONS

The *who* you are is far more difficult for an interviewer to determine, and some of the tactics widely used can be tricky to handle from your side of the desk. Remember, though, that the person facing you is trying to evaluate such intangibles as: perceptiveness, imagination, flexibility, integrity, diplomacy, poise, self assurance, objectivity, judgment, social awareness, and even the warmth or lack of it in your personality. It is a hard job, and some of the questions you may consider most irrelevant will be asked in an attempt to get at those qualities.

There are as many versions of these "who" questions as there are interviewers, and it is literally impossible to anticipate which ones will come up in any particular interview. This chapter will discuss a few of the most troublesome and suggest how to answer them. The important thing is to be aware that they are coming and be ready for them.

Your best preparation for this part of the interview is an advance, in-depth analysis of yourself: your personal goals, ambitions, relationships with others, involvement in community affairs, interest in politics, travel, cultural subjects, and anything else you can think of that defines you *as a person.* Be sure that *you* know who you are, and think about the best way to present the real you in a favorable light. The questions to follow will perhaps trigger others for you, and you should write down a brief answer to each before you start facing interviewers. After you've done this, try to find someone who has considerable management experience (a family friend, a professor in your school's department of business administration, or perhaps a counselor in the placement office) to discuss your analysis and give you the kind of "as others see you" feedback that will strengthen the good impression you want to make at interview time.

No matter what questions are asked, a good rule of thumb is to answer each one as honestly as you can, but not feel obliged to reveal things you consider too personal. Instead, deflect the intrusive part of the query by giving an indirect answer that focuses on something positive. This is not unlike the tactic much used by politicians when they skirt a controversial issue by addressing themselves to a safer, more favorable one.

Again, *Be Yourself!* If you must duck an issue or ignore a weakness when it is called for, do so, but be sure it is the *real* you the interviewer sees. Remember, too, that if the job calls for personal qualities you don't have, the job is not for you. You will be ahead of the game to recognize that fact. No amount of misrepresentation is going to make you right for that particular job, and if you were to land it, you would only be letting yourself in for future trouble.

Because there are so many varieties of the "who" questions, the examples given are limited to some of the most typical. For a more complete listing of questions frequently asked, see Appendix D.

"Tell me about yourself." Now, *there* is a question! Just what is

WHAT DO RECRUITERS SEEK?

The College Placement Council, in a booklet entitled "So You're Looking For A Job?", describes sixteen traits employers frequently seek in candidates:

1. **Ability to Communicate.** Do you have the ability to organize your thoughts and ideas effectively? Can you express them clearly when speaking or writing? Can you present your ideas to others in a persuasive way?

2. **Intelligence.** Do you have the ability to understand the job assignment? Learn the details of operation? Contribute original ideas to your work?

3. **Self-Confidence.** Do you demonstrate a sense of maturity that enables you to deal positively and effectively with situations and people?

4. **Willingness to Accept Responsibility.** Are you someone who recognizes what needs to be done and is willing to do it?

5. **Initiative.** Do you have the ability to identify the purpose for work and to take action?

6. **Leadership.** Can you guide and direct others to obtain the recognized objectives?

7. **Energy Level.** Do you demonstrate a forcefulness and capacity to make things move ahead? Can you maintain your work effort at an above-average rate?

8. **Imagination.** Can you confront and deal with problems that may not have standard solutions?

9. **Flexibility.** Are you capable of changing and being receptive to new situations and ideas?

10. **Interpersonal Skills.** Can you bring out the best efforts of individuals so they become effective, enthusiastic members of a team?

11. **Self-Knowledge.** Can you realistically assess your own capabilities? See yourself as others see you? Clearly recognize your strengths and weaknesses?

12. **Ability to Handle Conflict.** Can you successfully contend with stress situations and antagonism?

13. **Competitiveness.** Do you have the capacity to compete with others and the willingness to be measured by your performance in relation to that of others?

14. **Goal Achievement.** Do you have the ability to identify and work toward specific goals? Do such goals challenge your abilities?

15. **Vocational Skills.** Do you possess the positive combination of education and skills required for the position you are seeking?

16. **Direction.** Have you defined your basic personal needs? Have you determined what type of position will satisfy your knowledge, skills and goals?

it that the interviewer really wants to know about you? Well, it certainly is not your life story, fascinating though it may be. What he or she is trying to find out is "what is there about you that will make you a good employee?" Put in those terms, it is easier to handle. You know why you would work well in the operation, so address yourself to that topic. A general "I've always liked to work with people" (now *there* is an answer — as broad and "say-nothing" as the question!) just will not do. This is much better: "As long as I can remember, I have been fascinated by television commercials and printed ads. Even as a child, I made up sales slogans and tried them out on my friends. In college, my job as advertising manager of the campus newspaper taught me a lot about working with people. Now that I have my degree in advertising, it's exciting to look forward to working with a firm like yours, which has such a good track record for reading the public's taste and shaping buying habits." You have turned an open-ended question into a focused, positive restatement of your qualifications; you have restated your interest in that particular company; and you have added the qualities of imagination, enthusiasm, and perception. You have also told the interviewer specifically how you work well with people. That fills in quite a few of those "who" blanks!

"What are your major strengths?" Watch out for this one. You will want to be assertive enough to show self-confidence and drive without assuming a "know-it-all" or "hotshot" arrogance. A tall order, and resorting to humility is not suggested. But, by making your answer relevant to the job opening, and by citing past performance in other situations, you can strike the right tone. "I am flexible and very open to change" may tell the interviewer you have one of the qualities the employer values, but it may *also* convey the message that you lack perseverance and are likely to go off in all directions rather than sticking to a chosen course. "I function well in work that allows for change, and can frequently suggest improvements in procedures, as when our campus paper suffered a decline in advertising sales and I came up with a revised layout and new sales approach that brought revenue up by 45 percent." Your confidence is now based on proven ability. By being flexible within a given situation, you could envision a creative solution to a problem. If you have other strong points, talk about them in the same self-assured manner, giving illustrations.

"What is your greatest weakness?" On the face of it, this question asks you to admit to a failing at the very time you are trying hard to accentuate the positive. Happily, you can do both. "I get bogged down in details," is negative. But you can temper this potential weakness by saying: "Because attention to details sometimes slows me down, I make a special effort to develop a clear overview. I carefully analyze how much of my attention is directed to details, to be sure that my time is spent wisely."

The fact that you are aware of your tendency towards being overly detailistic reflects maturity; the fact that you think and do something about it indicates that you will be just as careful once you are employed. If you have worked out *this* problem, you can be expected to recognize and solve other job-related problems. Once again, you have turned a sticky question into an opportunity to show judgment, one of the most important of the "who" qualities.

A word of warning: If there are personal weaknesses you can not turn around like this, *do not mention them*. But *do* make a mental note that if they seem important in the job under discussion, then it well might not be for you. For instance, if you have an uncorrected memory weakness and details bore you senseless, you would be miserable in a job requiring a vast store of detailed information instantly at hand. You are better off looking elsewhere for a job concerned with broader aspects of your chosen field.

"Where do you see yourself ten years from now?" This frequently asked question can be a tough one to answer well. Appear too ambitious, and the interviewer may see you as just another "whiz kid" college grad out to conquer the world. On the other hand, giving no indication of long-range goals may brand you as aimless, with no clear sense of direction. Either pitfall can be avoided by taking the line that "Ten years from now, I want to have added good, solid experience to my educational foundation and be among the best in my profession." You can imply — or even flatly state — that this employer offers just such experience, which is what makes the open position especially attractive to you. Of course, the interviewer may probe further to determine your level of aspiration. In that case, cooperate by increasing the specificity of your response.

"What do you do in your spare time?" This one is not as irrelevant as you might think. True, your time away from work is your own. Yet employers often want to know if you are involved in community or cultural affairs, to what extent (will they interfere with job responsibilities?), how important sports and physical activities are to you, whether you are well read and keep up to date on world and local affairs, and other interests that will help fill in the "who" picture.

The key here is to try to show a spread of interests — from three to eight, depending on how demanding they are of your time. Show interests which reflect a well-rounded personality. Obviously, an interest like "going to the movies" is not going to create that image. But you *can* talk about an interest in the theater, including movies, and balance that with your favorite sport or volunteer work or literary pursuit. You should also indicate the degree of your interest in each activity.

These representative "who" questions and answers will give you an idea of how to help the interviewer form a favorable impression of you. Before you set out on interview rounds, it will be to your definite advantage to think through answers to each of the questions discussed above, as well as those listed in Appendix D. Keep in mind that some personal questions — those concerning family planning, personal relationships, personal finances and the like — may well be illegal if they have no direct bearing on job qualifications. But you are unlikely to have control over the questions asked, and it is far better to give an answer in the "turn around" manner demonstrated above, than to refuse one, and risk confrontation with the interviewer.

THE "WHY" FACTORS

As to the *why* part of the interview, your job from the moment you enter the interview room will be to project the *you* that will make it obvious you should be hired. Regardless of how well you perform that job, however, there must be a final evaluation by the interviewer based on everything you have revealed about yourself, plus things other than *what* and *who* you are that must be taken into consideration.

One important factor may well be your willingness or lack of it to start at or near minimum salary and job level, and work up. If you are faced with this question, remember that most entry-level jobs are going to be bottom-rung positions in your climb up the success ladder. How you respond to this type of questioning will depend on your own evaluation of the job. Chapter 12 discusses just how you can make that evaluation.

Then, there is that intangible factor, "chemistry." You may meet every requirement, have impeccable references, come across as an admirable and likable human being, and still not meet the "one of us" test. The interviewer simply may not relate well to your personality. Aside from being aware of the personal reaction taking shape between you and your interviewer, there is not much you can do to influence "chemistry." There is no way to safely second-guess on this score. Those who try nearly always end up in a quagmire of

IMPORTANT FACTORS IN THE SELECTION
OF COLLEGE GRADUATES FOR EMPLOYMENT*

Of special interest to college students, parents, faculty members and counselors is the relative importance of various factors which employers consider in selecting college graduates for employment. In other words, how do recruiters determine which applicants are best qualified?

Respondents were asked to rank, in order of importance, six factors which are commonly considered by employers in the selection of college graduates. Responding employers ranked the six factors from 1 to 6, with number one representing greatest importance.

It was noted in tabulating the responses that some employers ranked certain factors high and others ranked them lower. The **average rankings** in the following table are, therefore, only general indications of relative importance.

	FIELDS OF STUDY IN COLLEGE			
FACTORS CONSIDERED IN THE EMPLOYMENT OF COLLEGE AND UNIVERSITY GRADUATES	Engineering and Other Technical	Accounting and Bus. Admin.	Liberal Arts and Other Non-Tech.	All Fields of Study
	Order / Avg. Rank	Order / Avg. Rank	Order / Avg. Rank	Order / Avg. Rank
Personal qualifications including maturity, initiative, enthusiasm, poise, appearance and the ability to work with people.	(1) 1.97	(1) 1.73	(1) 1.52	(1) 1.75
Scholastic qualifications as shown by grades in all subjects or in a major field.	(2) 2.37	(2) 2.43	(2) 2.64	(2) 2.47
Specialized courses relating to particular field of work.	(3) 2.72	(3) 3.07	(5) 3.99	(3) 3.22
Kind and amount of part-time or summer employment while in college.	(4) 3.72	(4) 3.89	(4) 3.85	(4) 3.82
Experience in campus activities, especially leadership and participation in extra-curricular life.	(5) 4.31	(5) 3.94	(3) 3.60	(5) 3.96
General or liberal arts courses designed to provide a broad and cultural background.	(6) 5.54	(6) 5.41	(6) 5.05	(6) 5.35
Number of companies responding.	166	190	146	215

*Source: The Endicott Report, 1976. Published and copyrighted by The Placement Center, Northwestern University, Evanston, Illinois.

conflicting images, the strongest of which is that of someone who has no strong self-image.

The more quickly you create a warm, amiable feeling between you and the interviewer, the faster you'll be able to be yourself. If you fail to develop rapport quickly, you'll probably be nervous and unable to express yourself as well as you might when you're more relaxed. Naturally, most people will be somewhat anxious going into an interview. This is normal and to be

REASONS WHY EMPLOYERS DO *NOT* OFFER
JOBS TO CERTAIN GRADUATES*

Employers were asked to respond to the following question: "What are the most common reasons for NOT offering a job? In other words, what negative factors most often lead to rejection?"

A total of 166 employers responded. Negative factors are listed below in order of frequency of mention.

Factors	Frequency of Mention
Negative personality or poor impression: More specifically, lack of motivation, ambition, maturity, agressiveness or enthusiasm	110
Inability to communicate—Poor communication skills	62
Lack of competence—Inadequate preparation	56
Low grades—Poor grades in major field	38
Unidentified goals	32
Unrealistic expectations	28
Lack of interest in the type of work	25
Unwillingness to travel or to relocate	23
Poor preparation for the interview	14
Lack of work experience	10

*SOURCE: The Endicott Report, 1980. Published and copyrighted by The Placement Center, Northwestern University, Evanston, Illinois.

expected. If the nervousness persists, however, it can be detrimental to the outcome of your interview. The more self-assurance you project, the more credibility you'll establish.

JASON ROBERTSON
*HOW TO WIN IN A JOB INTERVIEW**

*Copyright © 1978 Reprinted by permission of Prentice-Hall, Inc., Englewood Cliffs, New Jersey

The only way to deal with the "chemistry" at work during your conversation is to *be yourself*, but use every technique you can master to be your *best* self. If that phrase is beginning to sound repetitive, it's only because it embodies a principle that simply cannot be overstated.

HOW YOU ARE RATED

Employers use many different rating forms to record their appraisals of entry-level aspirants. There are probably as many different approaches as there are employers; perhaps more, as some large employers have different versions for various divisions or departments. All, however, share in common their attempt to portray a total picture of applicants so that comparisons and decisions can be made as the recruiting season progresses.

An example of one of those forms can be found in Figure 8.1. This one is from an advertising agency, but substitute any other function for the word "Advertising" in the Motivation rating (item 10), and it is typical of most such appraisal forms.

WHAT YOU WILL WANT
TO KNOW

In the course of compiling your Job Search Control file (Chapter 4), you have already determined in your own mind which companies offer the best opportunities. No amount of advance research, however, can supply the specifics you must have in order to evaluate a job offer intelligently. It is in the interview that you will be able to ferret out that information.

James E. Burke, chairman of the board, Johnson & Johnson, advises: "I would try to isolate those companies that I felt were doing the best job in achieving their apparent goals. I emphasize the 'I' because while others can be helpful in giving advice, the key is how the individual views the institution and its worth."

The first step is to ask yourself some questions. These are summarized by Jeannette Gadomski, assistant vice president, The Bank of New York:

"The most successful interviews occur when the job-seeker is generally well-informed about the company and has some general idea of the role he or she may serve. Although the entry level job-seeker often feels disadvantaged by lack of experience or specific

CANDIDATE EVALUATION FORM

CANDIDATE _____

SCHOOL _____ INTERVIEWER _____ DATE _____

EVALUATION FACTORS

WEAK	BELOW AVERAGE	AVERAGE	ABOVE AVERAGE	OUTSTANDING
1	2	3	4	5

INTERVIEWER'S SUMMARY

	1	2	3	4	5		1	2	3	4	5
1. Personal Appearance	☐	☐	☐	☐	☐	11. Involvement	☐	☐	☐	☐	☐
2. Articulation/Expressiveness	☐	☐	☐	☐	☐	12. Extracurricular Activities	☐	☐	☐	☐	☐
3. Interview Preparation	☐	☐	☐	☐	☐	13. Maturity	☐	☐	☐	☐	☐
4. Responsiveness/Enthusiasm	☐	☐	☐	☐	☐	14. Judgment	☐	☐	☐	☐	☐
5. Persuasiveness	☐	☐	☐	☐	☐	15. Interpersonal Skills	☐	☐	☐	☐	☐
6. Decisiveness	☐	☐	☐	☐	☐	16. Social Amenities	☐	☐	☐	☐	☐
7. Perceptivity	☐	☐	☐	☐	☐	17. Manner/Chemistry	☐	☐	☐	☐	☐
8. Creativity/Imagination	☐	☐	☐	☐	☐	18. Overt Intelligence	☐	☐	☐	☐	☐
9. Analytical Facility	☐	☐	☐	☐	☐	19. Leadership Potential	☐	☐	☐	☐	☐
10. Motivation for Advertising	☐	☐	☐	☐	☐						

COMMENTS: (Continue on other side if necessary) _____

_____

_____

_____

_____

_____

_____

_____

	1	2	3	4	5
OVERALL EVALUATION	☐	☐	☐	☐	☐

Invite for interview   Hire

☐ YES   ☐ NO   ☐ YES   ☐ NO

INTERVIEWER'S SIGNATURE & TITLE _____

FIGURE 8.1

industry knowledge, one can begin the process of preparing for an interview by asking a few questions.

What is the business of this company?
Why am I interested in this business/company?

What experiences in my life can I relate to this business?

What do I know about my own personality — style, talents, which will make me a productive employee? (That is, am I analytical; sales-oriented; production-oriented; line or staff oriented? Do I write well? Communicate well? Manage others well?)

What do I know about the people who have been successful in this industry? How am I like them?

Once you have answered these for yourself, you are much better prepared for the time in the interview when you are asked whether you have any questions. If that does not happen, it's up to you to interject a polite "There are a few points I'd like to clear up before I leave." Do not hesitate to do so; you will be demonstrating initiative and interest.

What questions should you ask? Any that will give you a clearer picture of the company's long-range plans or objectives, especially as they impact on your area of interest, and that will more specifically define the job opening or training program.

When examining the wide range of jobs that are available or likely to be available, ask yourself: Where do I want to be, Where do I want to make a contribution, Where do I want to grow personally and professionally, in this complex, mobile, fast-moving, ever-changing world? Evaluate your choices in terms of:

a. Personal appeal. Know which options appeal to you most and know why they appeal to you.

b. Risks involved. Study the realities of the job market and assess the potential ease or difficulty of entering your chosen field.

c. Personal investment. Know what you must invest in terms of time, effort, energy, education, and training to enter a particular field.

d. Lifestyle. Be sure to understand the kind of personal and career lifestyle implied in each career option before you make your choice.

MARIE J. DE STENA
CAREER COUNSELOR
CAREER COUNSELING AND PLACEMENT OFFICE
FORDHAM UNIVERSITY

Keep your questions about the company itself short and general, and do not ask for information that is easily obtained from material readily available to the public. Instead, your questions should reveal all the research you have already done, and should be directed to the types of information you are not likely to be able to get elsewhere. "It is phenomenal the pleasant reaction the business executive has for the occasional individual who has the imagination, intuition, energy and desire to 'do homework' about the company or officers prior to an interview," says Leland T. Waggoner, C.L.U., senior vice president, Home Life Insurance Company.

Useful questions are listed below. Obviously, you should not ask any that do not interest you or for which an answer has no bearing on your evaluation of the potential employer or the open position. In short, do not ask questions merely because you think they will make you "look good." Rather, ask those that will increase your understanding of the employer, its people, the job, and future opportunities.

Company Goals

- Does the company contemplate introducing new products or expanding marketing operations?
- Are branches in other locations planned?
- Are headquarters likely to be relocated?

The Job Opening

- Is this job newly created? If not, has its function changed greatly in the last few years? How?
- Does it offer good promotional possibilities? (You will have to make this determination yourself to some extent, but it helps to know if others have moved up from the spot.)
- Is its scope limited to one department, or does it interact with others? (If it is a good vantage point from which to learn the overall operation, the chances of moving up are increased considerably.)
- Will it require you to travel? How much? Will you need a car?
- How many people staff the department in which you would work?
- To whom would you report? (Who will be your immediate and executive supervisors?)
- Is there a union involved? Would you have to join?

Other Company Policies Affecting
Your Development

- Is there a formal training program? Continuing education with tuition reimbursement? In-house seminars? A formal or informal mentoring system?
- Are there company-sponsored outside activities? Would you be expected to participate? Would you be permitted to participate?

Salary and Employee (Fringe) Benefits
Keep these questions for late in the interview. Ideally, they should not be brought up until a firm offer is made. But if near the end of the interview the subject has not been mentioned, and you are feeling good about the way things have gone, a polite inquiry as to salary range and employee benefits may serve to reinforce your serious interest in the job. If you are asked what salary you expect, avoid naming a specific figure. See Chapter 9 for details on how to negotiate the best deal for yourself.

How You Stand
What are your chances? *Don't ask*! Later in this book, you will find a discussion of some clues that will help you draw your own conclusions. But do not touch on this directly. You *can* indicate that you look forward to hearing further from your interviewer soon, thus indirectly expressing your expectation of favorable consideration.

YOUR OWN "WHO" QUESTIONS

Just as important to your evaluation of the job is the question of the organization's personality. And while some of *your* Who questions will be answered in the course of the interview, you will have to depend on your own awareness, perceptions, and judgments for answers to most. Following are some important clues to watch for.

About the Interviewer

- Are you being warmly and respectfully dealt with, or are you being impersonally processed?
- Were you kept waiting an unreasonable length of time with no satisfactory explanation or apology?
- Does the interviewer seem harried? Impatient?
- Are there constant interruptions?
- If coffee breaks or lunch come during interviews, are you invited to participate?

About the Offices

- Are they alive with activity, or deathly quiet?
- Are desks sloppy or neat to the point of perfection?
- Are all employees busy?

- Check the employee bulletin board if you can. Is it covered with rules and regulations, or does it seem responsive to human concerns?

About Potential Peers and Supervisors

- Do employees reflect tension?
- Do you see signs of nervousness at the appearance of a manager? Any "backstabbing" expressed in your presence? (Do as much eavesdropping as you can during waiting times or office tours.)
- Does everyone observe the same dress code? If so, is it one with which you would be comfortable?

If any one, or a combination, of these conditions leaves you feeling uneasy, it is a signal to look twice at the situation. It is in these surroundings and with these people that you may be spending the better part of your waking hours. If you will have trouble being yourself in this setting, it will be wise to find a more compatible environment.

> Don't take just anything, but do take anything reasonably related to what you are looking for. Ask about skills involved in the job. If they are skills which you will acquire that may be useful later, give the job serious consideration. Careers are built by banking skills. Each job, assuming it involves some skills, becomes the stepping stone to the next.
>
> STANLEY E. COHEN
> VICE PRESIDENT
> ADVERTISING AGE

TYPES OF INTERVIEWS

In the course of your job hunt, you may experience as many different interview techniques as the number of interviews you have. Which ones are used by each employer will depend on a number of variables, and you will feel more comfortable and better prepared if you are aware of the different types of interview situations you may encounter.

Usually, personnel department interviews are designed to assess your general biographical background and personality. Technical skills and knowledge are often determined by operating managers. Management potential is usually determined by a series of interviewers. If project management (or the team approach) is a dominant management characteristic of the company, you may face a group interview session. If stress is a part of the job requirement, you may be referred to a professional psychologist or put through a grueling "stress" interview.

The types of interviews most usually conducted are:

The Screening Interview

The objective here is to give the interviewer brief, but sufficient, information about you to determine whether you should have a full interview with someone closer to the hiring decision level. A good example is the campus recruiter who may screen a dozen or more students a day, but invite only two or three to visit the company for additional interviewing. You may be asked to complete an application form, even though you have already submitted your resume.

The screening interview is sometimes conducted by phone. If you find yourself being interviewed that way, try to project the same personality and enthusiasm you would show in a face-to-face interview. The overall impression you convey must be favorable enough to convince the caller that a personal meeting would be mutually beneficial.

The "Normal" Interview

In the most common, one-to-one, interview, you will be talking with an individual you may reasonably assume to be objective, tolerant of your point of view, and respectful of you as a person. The inter-relationship you develop in this conversation will be built on a free, give-and-take discussion, and the outcome will be based on both your best interests and those of the firm. Everything already said about being yourself applies most strongly in this situation. You will need to be relaxed, talk in an easy, natural manner, and keep in mind those "turn around" answers to the *who* questions — in other words, put your best self forward.

The Unstructured Interview

The unstructured interview can be extremely stressful if you are not ready for it. After an initial "Tell me about yourself," the inter-viewer simply sits back and waits for you to do just that, offering no response beyond an occasional "Is that so?" or "Yes?" The thing to do in this situation is to remember all the *what* and *who* questions most interviewers are interested in, then proceed to fill your narra-tive with these facts. Although you are not being questioned, act as though you were, making positive statements about your qualifica-tions and personality, being sure to relate all statements to the employer's requirements as you know them and to the specific job for which you are applying.

The Group Interview

While the group interview can be unnerving, if you remember that there are very good reasons for its use, you will be more comfortable with it. First of all, this is a time saver — yours as well as the employer's. If teamwork is important in the job being considered, your ability to function well in a group becomes a job requirement. This is your opportunity to demonstrate that ability. Some clues: listen closely to introductions and try to understand the "pecking order" within the group. Answer every question, looking at the person asking it, then follow with a short summary sentence directed to the person who heads the group.

The Serial Interview

In this situation, you meet with a succession of individuals selected to evaluate your candidacy. You'll know you are in for this sort of relay race if you're asked to be prepared to spend the morning or the better part of a day at the company. It is a commonly used procedure, and one not to be feared. Just keep your wits about you and treat each interviewer as though he or she were the first, repeating any information you may have already provided and trying for a good interrelationship with each one. Remember, a final decision is going to be reached by consensus. Therefore, it is important to impress each of your interviewers favorably.

The Stress Interview

The "stress" interview can be an ordeal. Happily, it is not used very often. If you should run into it, you are well advised to recognize what is happening and proceed accordingly. Sometimes this method is used because the job itself entails a good deal of stress. Sometimes it is used for no other reason than that the interviewer happens to be a frustrated martinet who enjoys shooting questions at you rather than approaching your meeting as a civil exchange of information.

The stress such interviewers apply is most often apparent in their line of questioning. But they also have (sometimes tortuous) methods which they use along with their highly probative, tense approach to interviewing. One of their favorites is to constantly stare at you, with virtually no letup. They can also make you feel uncomfortable with elongated silences, or by deliberately interrupting or distracting you, possibly causing you to lose your train of thought.

Here is an example of stress dialogue:

Q. What made you decide to go to college?

A. My parents never had the opportunity and wanted their children to go.

Q. Weren't you able to make that decision on your own?

A. Yes, I think so, but there were family finances to consider.

Q. Well, then, why didn't you go to work instead?

A. My parents and I decided that in the long run a college education would qualify me to make more money.

Q. In other words, college was just a way of making more money?

A. No, that wasn't all we had in mind.

Q. Well, then, just why did you decide to go to college, which, if you recall, was my first question? (Asked with heavy sarcasm.)

Aside from keeping your wits about you and trying to foresee such traps, about all you can do is to live through this trial; ride it out in the hope that it will get you to a later, normal interview. If nothing else, you will have made a positive impression simply by hanging in there, and you will have learned something about the *who* of the hiring organization.

SECOND AND SUBSEQUENT INTERVIEWS

Second and subsequent interviews are often conducted to confirm (or challenge) a first-interview impression. Other times, they are simply to obtain additional information.

Not surprisingly, follow-up interviews are handled almost the same as the first, except that as you reach successively higher levels, the conversation changes character somewhat. Listen carefully, at each level, for policy positions, corporate-level objectives and goals, management philosophy, and perhaps some significant organization problems.

For each interview, you should prepare as carefully as for the first, reviewing your notes from those that went before and reviewing company materials and press clippings you've accumulated for your Job Search Control file.

If the same person interviews you more than once, handle each meeting as though it were the first. Repeat everything, even when questions are repetitious. Do not take it for granted that the interviewer remembers everything that has been discussed before. Moreover, there may have been an intervening pre-employment test or assessment by someone else which has given rise to further questions.

The most important interview will be with the person who is your prospective supervisor. Here, "chemistry" and "gut reaction" are of prime importance. Get ready for this one by reviewing the basic functions of the job, how it fits into the organization, and the duties and responsibilities that will be yours. Any prospective boss will have to be impressed by such thoughtful preparation as shown by insightful questions, reasoned observations of problems that have been defined, and an evident understanding of the manager's challenges, problems, and operating requirements.

"I think the most important characteristics that employers will be looking for when interviewing new employees are enthusiasm, commitment, and motivation," says Esther Peterson, former president Jimmy Carter's special assistant for consumer affairs. "In most jobs, skills in verbal and written communication are important as well as analytical abilities. Prospective employees who come into an interview with a basic understanding of the organization's goals and how they can make an effective contribution should have an edge on those who have not taken the time to research or give thought to the organization's mission and how they can fit into it."

Thomas P. Murphy, director of the Office of Executive Personnel and Career Development, U.S. Office of Education, adds: "Any sign of life and imagination and willingness to work will help to create a favorable impression. A fair dose of humility will go a long way in convincing the interviewer that the individual will be able to hang in long enough to be successful."

Whit Hobbs, creative consultant to *The New Yorker Magazine* and Sperry Corporation, as well as a monthly columnist in *ADWEEK*, highlights the need for an appropriate mindset when he says: "Bring the right attitude with you. Not 'Tell me all about the fringe benefits.' Rather, 'I know how busy and harassed you are; sure, I'm green and inexperienced, but I'm eager as hell, I can work hard and learn fast, what I've been given to do I've always done well, I'm savvy, I've got a few special skills that I think you'll find useful; so it occurs to me that with a minimum of fuss I'll be able to accept responsibility and help you lighten your load.' What I can do for you, rather than what you can do for me."

Above all, do not suddenly become overly eager to please or

try to second-guess the manager and put on an act. If you misread the interviewer, you will blow your chances. Furthermore, an act simply cannot be maintained over the long run. Again, be your best self.

INTERVIEW SCHEDULING

Try not to schedule interviews with highly preferred employers at the start of your job-seeking efforts. As you go along in the interviewing process, you'll gain experience, self-confidence, and sharpened skills. Of course, if a preferred employer responds to your application earlier than you expected, don't hesitate to get back quickly and arrange for an interview.

Is there a "best" time of day to be seen? Should you try to be the first interviewee in the morning (because you believe the interviewer has maximum receptivity at the start of the day), or the last (with the hope that you'll outshine the competition and leave a memorable impression)? If you can't arrange to be either first or last, are you better off being interviewed before lunch or after?

The amount of debate on this subject indicates the diversity of opinion. The fact is, among the great majority of interviewers the time you're seen is unlikely to make a difference. But even if it did, there's no way for you to know whether one time or another will be in your favor with a particular interviewer, or even if it matters at all. So direct your energies to the many other aspects of your job search, and don't fret about the time of day your interviews are held.

IN BRIEF

In this chapter, you have seen that interviews are really all about the following: Things the interviewer will want to know about you; things you will want to know about the employing organization; things you will want to know about the job; and frequently used types of interview techniques.

It remains now to examine how best to prepare for interviews and how to get through them successfully — and that's what Chapter 9 is all about.

9

Successful Interviews

No matter how much you know about interviews, there is still the fearsome matter of getting through them successfully. No matter what your chosen field, to do this you must be a *salesperson*. You are going to have to *market* this product that is *you*, and that boils down to mastering skills in the mechanics of interviewing.

Before getting into specifics, however, recognize one simple fact: your ego is going to be squarely on the line each time you face an interview. It will be inflated at times, battered at others. Your best protection against the elation/depression seesaw is to realize that it is an integral part of the job hunting process. Then get a firm grip on your self-esteem and hang on to it! Your belief in yourself is vital in every interview situation. While it may be shaken by rejection (or even by those sleepless nights of waiting to learn the outcome), remembering that interviews are exploratory conversations and cannot all result in job offers will help restore it in short order. It will help, too, to know that you have done your background preparation thoroughly, have gone into each interview well prepared, and have performed to the best of your ability. The importance of this approach to the job-seeking process is well summed up by Charles G. Bluhdorn, chairman of the board, Gulf+Western Industries: "There are no secrets to finding the best job at the right company. The most important ingredients are clearly defining your career goals, doing the homework necessary to find the right company, and showing the self-confidence gained from knowing your strengths."

BEFORE THE INTERVIEW

The first step in preparing for any interview is to review every bit of information in your Job Search Control file about the employing organization and the job opening. Go over everything as many times as it takes to enable you to talk with ease about the key employer knowledge you have. Be sure you can go into the interview with a solid bank of information in your head, not just in your file back home.

Then write out the questions you will want to ask about the organization and the specific job for which you are applying. Some of these will be answered in the give-and-take of conversation, but you should have firmly in mind the clarifications you will need to make an intelligent evaluation. Remember, of course, that these questions should not concern any information easily available from outside sources; asking such questions is one sure way to shoot down that well-informed impression you are trying to create. Again, review your questions thoroughly so that they become a natural part of your thinking about this particular employer and this particular job.

Now apply that same procedure to all that you know about your own background. Memorize your resume and its cover letter. You should have a clear, sharp picture of all your qualifications and be able to talk about them without having to search through the resume itself. When it comes time to answer the "what you are" and "what you've done" questions, you should be ready with quick, sure replies.

As for the "who you are" part of the interview, this is where a beforehand self-analysis comes in. Try to develop an accurate, objective self-view. Re-read the section on "Putting Your Resume Together" in Chapter 5, and go over the fifty questions in Appendix D. Study the "turn around" techniques discussed in Chapter 8; then write out answers to the sticky *who* questions, employing those techniques. Become familiar enough with your answers so that they flow naturally.

Try to answer each question as concisely as you can. This does not necessarily mean one word, or even one sentence. Take a lesson from television commercials: see yourself as the advertiser who must sell the audience (your interviewer) your abilities, talent, and personality with very little time in which to do it. Go over each answer to be sure you've made the best possible choice of words.

THE ART OF VERBAL COMMUNICATION

Enough preparation? Not by a long shot! What will it matter if you know just what you want to say and all the questions you want to ask if you do not know how to communicate them effectively? Very little. So, the next step in your advance preparation is to learn, improve on, and polish your verbal communication skills.

Your job now is to become so skilled a conversationalist that you will produce a clear, strong, favorable impression and affirmative responses from your interviewer. *What* you say is important, of course. The "turn around" technique is one good example of communicating basic information in words carefully chosen to create the best impression. Familiarity with all necessary facts is another.

However, even the right words can be lost if they are spoken in the wrong way at the wrong time. The right information communicated in the wrong way can cause negative rather than positive results. And, sometimes words lose all import in light of the speaker's overall manner. Non-verbal attributes can be so strongly negative that they wipe out positive statements. So, *how* you communicate in the interview ranks right alongside *what* you communicate.

One of the most important factors in good communication is careful listening. Don't jump the gun in replying, even when an answer is on the tip of your tongue. Respond to each question only when you're sure the interviewer is completely finished posing it and you are certain you understand just what is being asked. Never interrupt with a premature reply; it works against you in two ways. First, you may misinterpret the interviewer's question, simply because you did not hear the end of it. Second, you make a poor impression on the interviewer for not having had the courtesy to wait for a complete question.

If you do not quite grasp the meaning of a word or phrase, *ask.* For example, interviewer: "During your tenure as club treasurer, did you ever experience a shortfall?" Interviewee: "Would you please define 'shortfall' for me?" Another way of doing this is to rephrase the question before replying; if there is a misunderstanding on your part, the interviewer has an opportunity to correct it. Example: interviewee responds, "Do you mean did we find ourselves with less income than anticipated?"

If a question is unexpected, and catches you short, it's okay to take a slight pause in order to couch your reply in thoughtful, concise terms. Even when you are so well prepared that time for reflection isn't necessary, it's wise occasionally to give the appearance of thoughtful consideration. The impression you want to convey is self-confidence based on careful thought.

Above all, speak clearly and distinctly. Modulate your voice so that sentences do not drop to a murmur at the end or boom so loudly that sheer volume becomes a distraction. Remember, too, that the tone of your voice can indicate warmth or the lack of it; inject as much enthusiasm as you can, and if humor is appropriate, use it (but this is no place to be "cute"!). If a point of view is called for, don't hesitate to state your own, but be careful not to go overboard and portray yourself as being closed to other views. The last thing you want to engage in at this time is an argument on principles or theories. A thoughtful, "That's an interesting point of view. You've given me something to think about" gets you off the hook and flatters your interviewer without compromising your own stand.

If you should run into an unexpected question for which you have no answer, *admit so.* You can turn a deficiency into an asset, however, by the simple technique of evidencing interest in the missing information and showing enthusiasm when you say, "I'll have to look into that and get back to you tomorrow (or this afternoon, or any specific time)." Then, be sure you follow through and furnish the answer when promised.

If you feel the interviewer doesn't understand what you've said after you've given your best answer to a question, go over it again in slightly different terms. Don't be longwinded, just be certain you've made your point in a way that cannot be misunderstood.

OVERQUALIFIED AND UNDERQUALIFIED

Almost every applicant, at one time or another, comes up against the "over- or under-qualified roadblock." Neither, however, should be viewed as the end of the road in the interview situation. If you are told you are overqualified, never leave it at that. Ask politely if there is a job available now or one that will come up in the foreseeable future that will use your qualifications. Another alternative is to explain that you are willing to start at a lower level in order to gain experience.

In the case of an "underqualified" judgment, you can review your education and experience, along with any personal strong points, and add that you are eager to close the qualification gap with on-the-job training.

In either case, try to leave with the understanding that your application will be kept in the company's open files.

APPEARANCE COUNTS!

All the time you are employing verbal techniques, non-verbal communication is going on that can reinforce what you say or cancel out your words completely. For example, your appearance will tell the interviewer much about you as a person. Dean Donald G. Hileman, College of Communications, University of Tennessee, counsels: "Your appearance by the clothes you wear, your mannerisms, your facial expressions, in fact, all of the non-verbal signs are just as important as the words you use in an interview."

A sign at the entrance to the interviewing rooms at the College of Engineering, University of Wisconsin-Madison, has this sage advice: "You will never get a second chance to make a good first impression."

Good personal grooming is a "must" in any interview situation. No employer wants to hire a slob! That means your nails must be clean, face well scrubbed, hair neatly arranged. You have to look clean and smell clean, or you are very likely to strike out. Oral hygiene is especially important. Perfume, after-shave, colognes, should be used in moderation. You may take these things for granted (hopefully, you do), but you would be surprised how many applicants appear for an interview with one or more failings in personal cleanliness.

Beyond that, the way you are dressed not only reflects your personal tastes, but is also an indication of judgment. If you show up in attire that is completely inappropriate, the interviewer will probably conclude that you are not likely to exercise very good judgment in actual work situations. That doesn't mean, however, that colorless, ultraconservative dress is your only recourse. On the contrary, it could rule you out as unimaginative in a field where a certain sense of style and flair may be a prerequisite. Keep in mind that while there are no hard and fast rules on how to dress for an interview, there is the guiding principle of dressing in a manner appropriate to the employer to which you are applying. If you are fortunate enough to have had the chance to observe employees on the job, while visiting a potential employer for a student orientation program, or remembering how your on-campus interviewer dressed, this is not much of a problem. But most often, it is not possible to know in advance. When in doubt, therefore, *go conservative.* If you are not sure what "conservative" means, check with your placement counselor, read through the Brooke's Brothers catalog, visit a local high-fashion store, talk to a classmate who attended a prep school.

Men should wear ties and jackets. Women are best off in suits, dresses, or coordinated blouses and skirts. Clothing should be clean and pressed. Shoes should be shined. It is doubtful that many applicants fail to get hired because they show up in a suit and wear low-key accessories. The converse, however, is eminently more likely!

"Initially, a prospective employer will judge you by your appearance," advises Carl W. Menk, president and chief executive officer of Boyden Associates, executive recruiters. "That may seem like an artificial, surface criterion, but don't discount its importance. While you're sitting there in your scuffed shoes and stained collar, the employer will be thinking, 'Will this person be able to get the respect of our most difficult distributor? Will he or she have the polish to entertain our clients with confidence? Will the board be impressed?' "

Hair can be a difficult issue for men. For years, some collegians have been practicing "hair hype." While employers have differing viewpoints, no job seeker was ever rejected because he did not sport a beard. But lots of managements see no "socially redeeming value" in a large mop on top, or elaborate (or worse, untrimmed) face fuzz. It is your privilege to wear your hair any way you wish, and you can dress as slovenly as you please, but realize that these things will take their toll on the number of job offers you get.

Syndicated columnist and noted raconteur Art Buchwald offers this guidance: "My advice to youthful job-seekers is to always wear a tie, comb your hair and shave — if you are a boy. If you are a girl — wear a nice dress and try to look like Debbie Boone."

NON-VERBAL COMMUNICATION

Once inside the door, non-verbal communication comes through in everything from your initial handshake (beware the "dead fish" variety), to your facial expressions, and the way you sit in your chair. Especially in the beginning days of your job search, interviews are almost sure to cause tenseness, some of which will disappear as you go through the experience many times. Those first few times out, however, you should concentrate on appearing relaxed — not casual, just relaxed.

There are ways you can reflect a comfortable, at-ease attitude. For example, if a previous applicant has pushed the chair back so that it is at an awkward angle and you have trouble looking at your interviewer directly, ask politely if you may move it, or do so in an unobtrusive way without asking. A small matter, but one which shows you are relaxed enough about the situation to be sure small details do not get in the way of the business at hand.

Your facial expressions will play an important part in the interview, so keep them pleasant most of the time, flexible enough to show positive reaction to points made during the conversation, and in tune with the gist of the talk. When humor lightens the mood, respond with a smile; when things turn serious, let your face reflect thoughtful, sincere interest. Whenever possible, let reserved enthusiasm shine through your expression as well as your words.

Even the way you sit helps your interviewer size you up. Keeping arms and legs tightly crossed advertises inner tension. The kicking motion of a crossed leg is another tipoff that you are not really relaxed. Playing with a pen or pencil betrays nervousness. Slouching in your chair may depict you as just plain lazy, or it could say you are making an exaggerated effort to appear casual. On the other hand, a stiff, upright perch on the edge of your chair may suggest that you are so uptight that you are preparing for instant flight. All these postures should be avoided. Instead, assume a natural, easy position, resting your arms on the chair arms or holding them at ease with your hands in your lap.

Remember that your body speaks for you, so train it to speak favorably.

A visual presentation — something tangible brought with you to the interview — can be a very important part of your non-verbal communications. Visual presentations can be comprised of many kinds of things: byline articles that appeared in the school paper, publicity in connection with any prizes or awards you've won, special letters of commendation, even high-scoring papers on which the professor wrote "Bravo." Evidence of work achievements can also work well for you: doubling paper route customers, surpassing production quotas, increasing the summer shipping-room job efficiency by 20 percent. The list is endless. As appropriate, offer these to your interviewer, but do not be overly aggressive about doing so. If you detect lack of interest in them, back away. But be prepared by having them with you at every interview.

Last, but certainly not least, is the business of eye contact. A great deal is made of this in advising applicants on good interview techniques. It is important! In any conversation we benefit from frequently looking the other person in the eye. There is one caution, however; do not fix the interviewer with a beady unstraying stare. It is uncomfortable for you both and very likely to put the interviewer off. If you find yourself doing this, try shifting your gaze to the bridge of his or her nose (it will appear you are making eye contact and there will be less strain on you), or glancing off to either side from time to time. The important thing is to let your interviewer know he or she has your undivided attention. If you get pleasure from sporting sun or darkly-tinted glasses, do not wear them during an interview. "Masked" applicants have trouble projecting sincerity, negatively affecting the rapport they are trying to establish.

PRACTICE MAKES PERFECT

With all the foregoing firmly in mind, your next step should be to acquire interview practice before you face the real thing. Ask a friend, your parents, a business acquaintance, or another student who is also job hunting — anyone who will be objective — to sit down and "role play" the interview situation. There is no better way to get rid of at least *some* of those pre-interview jitters than by going through the whole routine beforehand. And every mock interview should improve your performance, doing wonders for your self-confidence.

Before you begin your practice session, explain to the person who will play the part of the interviewer that you want feedback on your mannerisms as well as the quality of your spoken words. Be sure that person knows this is serious business and that you are not just clowning around. Impress your mock interviewer with the fact that you are counting on this exercise to help you avoid pitfalls when you face the real-life situation.

Some graduates-to-be find it useful in practicing interviews to set up all sorts of adverse conditions so they will be ready for whatever they encounter. For instance, you might pretend that telephone calls constantly interrupt the interview. Or have your practice interviewer challenge some of your responses. In other words, let this practice be as far from ideal as you can make it so that if you are later in the "hot seat," you will be better prepared to react smoothly.

Another very useful technique is the use of a tape recorder. Keep it going through all your role plays. Listen to the playback for voice qualities. Try to judge for sincerity, warmth, and tone. Ask yourself if those carefully planned answers flow as naturally as they should. Often, the first taping or two cause the fledgling interviewee nightmares! Problems include choppy delivery, lots of "er's" and "ah's," disorganized responses, unenthusiastic projection. But you will be delighted with your improvement as you repeat the process and sharpen your presentation. If you are fortunate enough to have access to videotape equipment, use it to evaluate and improve body language, as well as verbal responses.

THE BIG DAY

Confirm each interview date and time several days in advance by phone. Be sure you know the name, title, and function of the person you will be meeting. If you have any question as to how to reach the interview office, ask for explicit directions when you call to confirm the appointment.

You will want to have a good breakfast or lunch, review all relevant material, and plan your day so you don't find yourself racing around trying to arrive on time. Gather the things you will need to take with you: an extra copy of your resume; a small notepad and pen; the names, titles, addresses, and phone numbers of your references; a list of the questions you want to ask (key words to trigger your memory will suffice); a note of the time, place, interviewer's name and title; and directions for reaching the office.

Plan your dress beforehand and leave home early enough not to be pressured by traffic or parking problems. If you should get to the interview site early, it is always a good idea to look the place over from the outside to get a feel for the neighborhood and the general features of the employer's facilities.

You should reach your interviewer's office on time, but not more than five or ten minutes early. Arriving too early may indicate a lack of planning to your interviewer. Introduce yourself to the receptionist or secretary, explain that you have an appointment, then sit down and wait. Don't be upset if your interviewer is behind schedule; it's fairly common, so be patient. If you are given an application form, fill it out neatly and completely. Maintain a restrained, politely social manner with the receptionist or secretary; don't be overly chummy, a joker, or a know-it-all. If informational pieces about the organization are in the reception area, look them over. You may pick up one or two facts you haven't seen before; at the least, they'll reinforce what you already know.

When you are ushered into the interviewer's office, thank the receptionist or secretary, introduce yourself, and shake hands. If your interviewer is female and you have any hang-ups about shaking hands with a businesswoman, get over them before you leave home! Remember that your non-verbal communication has already begun; keep your facial expression pleasant and your handshake firm.

Sit in the indicated chair and keep your opening conversation brief, social, and positive (this is not the time to complain about traffic or the scarcity of parking spaces). A complimentary comment on the plant or offices makes a good beginning and immediately establishes you as an observant person. If your resume has not preceded you, now is the time to offer a copy.

Smoke only if you are invited to do so, as more and more people object nowadays to smoking in their presence. If you are offered coffee or tea and you would like a cup, your best response is that you would be happy to join the interviewer if he or she is having one. Courtesy is always a respected trait.

Now that the interview is underway, all your preparation will begin to pay off. Practice sessions will have done away with some of the fear of a poor performance, and you should be able, after the first few minutes, to relax and find the experience interesting and informative.

> You should look forward to working for any individual and/or company that you interview with. If you don't, don't take their time or yours for an interview. Do your homework on the company and individuals with whom you will be interviewing. People are impressed that you have taken an interest in them and the company. It says "this is a special person" and the establishment of a good personal relationship should be the first step in an interviewing situation.
>
> DONALD G. HILEMAN, DEAN
> COLLEGE OF COMMUNICATIONS
> UNIVERSITY OF TENNESSEE

During the course of the interview, you will have occasion to use most of the techniques discussed, both verbal and non-verbal. There is one, however, for which you cannot prepare, and that is an awareness of the non-verbal communication *from* your interviewer. Without it, your own communication may falter and may not be as effective as it could be. For example, you will want to look for clues as to interest or lack of interest in a particular point so you can tailor your reply accordingly. If you see an indication of impatience, make your answer even more concise than you had planned, then ask if you have covered the point adequately. If, on the other hand, interest is shown through leading questions, expand a little more on the point under discussion. In other words, try to make a quick appraisal of this unknown person and react appropriately. Doing so will certainly enhance your interviewer's rating of your sensitivity and perceptivity.

Throughout your interview, keep in mind how important it is to talk about your skills and abilities in terms of the *employer's* needs. Too many applicants talk only of *their* interest in the job: why it is the kind of opportunity *they* have always wanted, how happy *they* know *they* would be on the job, why *they* are confident that the job fits *their* growth and development needs. In other words, an all "me," instead of "you," approach. Like a good advertisement (remember always, you are *marketing* yourself), you should sell yourself in terms of the market's (translation: employer's) wants and needs. *People get hired because employers perceive they will make contributions to their organizations, not because the applicants would like to personally gain from the relationship.*

Helpful advice for interview survival and success comes from Lawrence M. Baytos, vice president, Corporate Personnel, The Quaker Oats Company, who says: "Avoid the Tacky Ten:

1. Candidate does not make eye contact.
2. All questions relate to benefits/salary.
3. Candidate berates current boss/employer.
4. Candidate smokes without asking.
5. Candidate not knowledgeable of company's products.
6. Candidate is late for appointment.
7. Candidate dress is inappropriate.
8. Dead mackerel handshake syndrome.
9. Candidate rambles on with needless details.
10. Candidate cannot respond maturely to strengths/weaknesses self-assessment."

WHEN YOUR INTERVIEWER IS NOT A "PRO"

Occasionally, you may run into an inept interviewer, in which case you have a problem. Dealing with such a person can present a real challenge, one more easily met if you recognize beforehand that the possibility does exist and plan your strategy. Here are a few of the circumstances you could encounter and suggestions for coping with them:

INTERVIEW DO's AND DON'Ts

DO

–bring an extra copy of your resume to the interview.

–be prepared with carefully considered answers for questions about past changes, performance, motivation, and the like.

–learn as much as you can about the organization prior to the interview.

–be sincere and direct. Act naturally. Be your best self. Avoid putting on airs.

–help the interviewer develop a picture of your ambitions and expectations for the future, and be sure. these are consistent with your past accomplishments.

–dress appropriately, with reasonable conservatism.

–make it your business to be on time for each and every interview.

–sit back in your chair—at ease, but attentively.

–look your interviewer directly in the eye—and keep doing so from time to time during your interview.

–ask some questions about the organization. This demonstrates interest as well as giving you information.

–remember Mark Twain's words: "Always tell the truth, and you'll have less to remember."

DON'T

–light up a cigarette, cigar or pipe without first asking if you may smoke.

–haul out materials you've brought along (memos, commendations, reports, work samples, etc.) unless a clear opportunity presents itself.

–try to take over the interview. It's the interviewer's prerogative to guide the conversation. Of course, be responsive to each and every question.

–cancel an interview appointment unless absolutely necessary. And if you must cancel, do so yourself and offer to be available at several future dates.

–make a nuisance of yourself following the interview. Although a follow-up letter of "Thanks" is in order, avoid bombarding the interviewer with phone calls or other contacts.

–bring up minor questions in the first or preliminary interviews. There's plenty of time to find out about working hours, holidays, vacations, and so forth.

–conclude an interview by asking how you stand among applicants. You most likely won't get an answer, and you make yourself sound immature.

–be overly nervous. A frequent smile will serve you well.

–let discouragement show if you get the impression the interview is not going well. You have nothing to lose by continuing an appearance of self-confidence, and you just might cause a change in the interviewer's attitude towards you.

Your interviewer

- Misschedules your appointment (reset it).
- Keeps you waiting an unreasonably long time (explain to the secretary that you have another appointment and must re-schedule).
- Allows frequent interruptions by people walking in or by phone calls (politely ask if the interviewer would like to re-schedule your meeting for a less busy time).

- Freezes, due to interviewing inexperience (be patient and understanding; lead the discussion through each point on your resume and cover letter; you'll make a friend!).

- Talks incessantly (exhibit calm endurance until a lull, then edge in with your resume and cover letter data).

- Asks a question, then responds to your reply with protracted periods of silence (expand on your resume and cover letter, then ask if an elaboration of any point is desired — if still no answer, start asking the questions on your list).

- Asks one question after another in rapid-fire fashion (answer the last one first, then ask for a repeat of the others and continue until you have answered them all).

AS THE INTERVIEW
WINDS DOWN

When you are asked, "Are there any questions you would like to ask me?," it is a signal that the interview is coming to a close. If the conversation has not covered all your questions, be sure you ask them now. Then, briefly summarize your strong points as they relate to the job opening, and if you now feel you really want this job, say so. Express your interest in both the position and the company, as well as the hope that you will be considered favorably. As previously emphasized, do not ask what your chances are; you will be considered naive and unsophisticated if you do.

Be sure that when you leave the office, you have a clear idea of what to expect. Will there be further interviews? Testing? A physical examination? If the response is "We will let you know," try to determine an approximate length of time in which you may expect to hear about the next step or your status.

By this time, you and your interviewer are probably both on your feet. Close the interview by expressing appreciation for the time and interesting discussion, restating your interest in the job and that you will be looking forward to hearing further with regard to your application.

AFTER THE INTERVIEW

Immediately after the interview, you should look for a place to sit undisturbed long enough to make notes while the conversation is still fresh in your mind. Jot down your reactions, any specific information you have promised to furnish and the date it is due, points you may have overlooked or those you want to reinforce in your "thank you" letter, and any matters left unclarified that you will want to ask about later.

Regardless of the outcome of your meeting, write a "thank you" note expressing appreciation for the time given you. Not only is it courteous, but it works for you: in almost every well-structured organization, there is a procedure for bringing previous papers out of the file to be attached to current correspondence. So when your letter comes in, out comes your resume. This gives you one more exposure to a decision maker. Also, a new need may have developed since your meeting, and this becomes your chance to be considered again. Finally, should you be rejected now but considered at a future date, the filed record of your courtesy is one more point in your favor.

Your "thank you" letter should be as carefully composed as your resume and its cover letter. Try to be businesslike, with short, to-the-point sentences and sincere language. Check it more than once for grammar, spelling, and possible typing errors. Review key points you feel went well. Refer to the notes you made following the interview and incorporate any additional information you want the interviewer to have. Thank the interviewer for the time and courtesy given you, and use this letter to press gently for further action, re- state your interest in the job, and your expectation of hearing further within a definite time period. (Suggestion: Review the Mary Cappiola and Geraldine Wyckoff letters, Figures 7.7 and 7.8.)

EVALUATING THE INTERVIEW

To keep your Job Search Control file up to date and complete, you should write down your own evaluation of your prospects as soon as the interview is over. Of course there is no way to be certain how you stand unless you are told outright. But there are clues that can help you make an intelligent evaluation.

The first thing to bear in mind is that many interviewers will leave you feeling you cannot possibly miss getting the job! Unless there has been a concrete indication of that fact, dismiss it. The plain truth is that interviewers are generally skilled at concealing their reactions to candidates, and most are reluctant to give a face-to-face rejection. There are good reasons for this. First of all, they want to hold all applicants in reserve until the job is actually filled so that if first choices fall through they have some backup. Then, too, it is a difficult human relations situation when one person must tell an- other that he or she will not be hired.

Mentally review the interview, with the following indicators in mind:

Usually, the longer an interview goes on, the more interest there is in the applicant. Of course, if your interviewer was a compulsive talker, that may not be the case. Try to remember if the length of the interview was due to the scope of information covered or just plain ineptness at keeping it confined to the business at hand. Gauge, too, the enthusiasm your interviewer exhibited for your qualifications.

Another measure of success or failure is the amount of detailed explanation you were given of the employer's operations. If the job was explained in specifics and at length, or the training program was gone into in depth, with comments as to how it would benefit you as an employee, it is a good sign you were judged a serious candidate. If you were taken on an impromptu tour of work areas and introduced to employees, things should look even more promising.

More easily recognizable favorable indications include: asking your permission to check references; setting up further interviews or testing; giving you "inside" information to study; and asking when you will be available for work.

Whatever the overall impression you have of your standing, it should be noted in your Job Search Control file. In the course of going through several interviews, you will need to have a clear idea of each prospect.

ABOUT THOSE "NO'S"

Rejection is always difficult, whether in business, education, government, or personal life. In the realm of job hunting, however, you must recognize that being turned down may very well have nothing to do with your qualifications. The job may have been eliminated or absorbed in another one simply because of a general economic downtrend. Internal circumstances, such as a departmental budget cut, may result in the postponement of filling that particular opening. An unexpected promotion within the company may fill the vacancy. The job may be redefined in such a way that it calls for different qualifications. Or, the boss's nephew or niece may suddenly appear and land the job for which you applied. All sorts of things can happen to change the situation between the time of your interview and the time you hear the results.

A rejection letter should not, however, be the end of your contact. There is one more response you should make, and that is, ironically, another "thank you" letter. Keep the tone polite and

confine its contents to a "thank you for your time and consideration" and an expression of hope that you will again be considered
if something appropriate comes up. Your letter is another of the
"extras" that can make a big difference. Your file once more crosses
the desk of the interviewer, and your courtesy may make a long-
lasting impression. More than one successful person was first rejected
for the very job that eventually served as a beginning point for
success. (See Tony Lacki's letter, Figure 7.6.)

Of course, if you get what you feel are more than your share of
rejections, that is another matter. First of all, take a look at the jobs
for which you have been applying: are they at the right level? It may
be that you have set your sights too high or too low. What is called
for is a re-examination of both your own qualifications and the requirements of jobs you've been seeking. Be as realistic as you can
about this and try to determine if you need to shift direction. "Self-
analysis is difficult," notes William J. Driver, Commissioner of Social
Security. "Most of us resist looking at what we consider to be our
own inadequacies. Yet, only if we know ourselves can we respond
accurately to interview questions, choose among job offers, decide
to move to another location, and ultimately be of the most value to
ourselves and our employers."

After a good, hard look at your job expectations, turn to an
honest appraisal of your interview performance. Most deficiencies
can be corrected if you know what they are. Again, go to someone
who has had extensive management experience: your career
counselor, or a business professor whom you can trust for objective
answers, and ask for a critique of negative personal traits you may be
reflecting. You might want to go through another mock interview to
get first-hand feedback on how you have been presenting yourself.
Ask them to look for some of the problems that most commonly
account for job turndowns: inappropriate appearance; manners not
suitable for a business situation; indifference; evasiveness; excessive
nervousness; lack of poise or self-confidence. Once you have spotted
trouble areas, work on them long and hard before the next interview.

THE NEXT STEP

After each interview comes one of the most difficult parts of job
hunting: the wait! What to do? The answer is definitely *not* to sit
idly, staring at the telephone or haunting the mailbox. There are
positive ways to fill the gaps between interviews and those dreaded
waiting periods, and that is what Chapter 10 is all about.

IN BRIEF

It is vitally important to the success of your job search that you understand about preparing for the interview; learning verbal and non-verbal communication methods; practicing for the interview; facing the interview; post-interview techniques; and positive responses to rejections.

With all this under your belt, you are ready to learn how to cope with between-interview problems and opportunities.

10

What to Do between Interviews

With your job-search strategy in full operation, it's easy to sit back and feel it's only a matter of time before you will be comfortably settled in the job you have worked so hard to get. But it doesn't work that way. No matter how well planned your strategy or how vigorously you pursue it, there will probably be days and days of just plain waiting. That waiting can be frustrating, and possibly even destructive, unless you use it to reinforce all that has gone into this job of finding a job.

Consider the psychological effect of leaving an interview you believe went well, then sitting by the phone or haunting the mailbox for days, or even weeks, in anticipation of a callback, only to meet with dead silence. That can be pretty devastating! It becomes even more so if you have had more than one interview you feel might result in a job offer. As more time passes, you are likely to yield more and more to discouragement, and something akin to desperation may begin to set in. Each subsequent interview will find you less confident, with flagging enthusiasm and decreasing energy.

This is not a proper frame of mind in which to venture forth into the job market, to say the least.

A very vital part of your total job-search strategy, then, must be to plan that potentially-destructive, between-interview time intelligently so that it becomes a constructive force. While that may seem a tall order, it really is not that difficult.

MAKE YOUR IDLE TIME PAY OFF FINANCIALLY

Not only can you keep your morale high during job-hunting days, but you can actually make that time profitable financially — through temporary work. There are, however, several points to remember about interim jobs.

First, no matter what kind of work-for-pay you undertake, be sure to keep your hours flexible so that as interviews or callbacks come up you are free to pursue them. For that reason, part-time work is the most suitable during this period.

The most obvious is temporary part-time work for an office service or school department, but there are many other avenues open to you. For example, if you are good with a paintbrush or tools, try contracting for neighborhood housepainting or home repair jobs. By scheduling half days or only two or three work days during the week, you can leave yourself time for job-search activities. If your hobbies include crafts that produce marketable items, try selling them on a consignment basis to local shops or flea markets. If you are the outdoor type, line up customers for such chores as lawn cutting, gardening, swimming pool care, snow removal, pet walking, or even window washing. You might offer phone wake-up service for a fee. Another possibility is housesitting: some homeowners will pay a reliable sitter to live in their homes while they are away on vacations or business trips.

If you can utilize your education in part-time work, so much the better. Free-lance bookkeeping for small firms, copy editing, photography, or graphic arts work all are sources of income which can be fitted into a time schedule that leaves enough free time for your continuing job search efforts. If you have musical ability, part-time work for clubs, religious groups, restaurants, and the like are other examples. Investigate free-lance writing, marketing research projects in your field, or advertising space or product sales on a commission basis if any phase of communications or selling is your career objective. Hospital orderly work two or three days a week offers exposure to the medical field while you are waiting for that higher-level job. Private tutoring or part-time classroom instruction will utilize your education and strengthen your resume. Bill Haight, publisher of *National On-Campus Report*, advises: "Young people should amass experience away from the college environment to supplement their academic credentials. Experience with a part-time job (in a real-world setting) or in a small self-employment project will show the potential employer the applicant has at least some knowledge of the fact of life that real-world rewards must be earned by providing something of value to someone else."

In a *Journal of College Placement* article, "Part-time Student Employment: The Benefits to Students and Employers," authors Don L. Warrington (Director, Career Placement Services) and Janet M. Rives (Associate Professor of Economics), University of Nebraska at Omaha, had this to say about the value of part-time employment: "Job placement opportunities are greatly improved for students with part-time work experience. In many instances, placement with their present employer will result in their transition from part-time to full-time status after graduation. Those part-timers who seek full-time positions elsewhere will be effective in their job search because of their improved self-understanding and knowledge of the world of work (qualities which are highly valued by employers) and because of their established work histories. Additionally, graduates with these qualities are likely to make well-informed placement decisions and can command starting salaries higher than those individuals without prior, work-related experience."

In any part-time work, concentrate on *contacts* as well as the income you will be earning. Talk to employer customers or clients and full-time co-workers about your career goals. Referrals can come from the most unexpected sources, and you should be alert to every one of them.

While most prospective employers will fully understand a soon-to-be or recent graduate's desire and need to keep busy during the job-hunting period, it is a good idea to have phone contact numbers on your resume which are not associated with your part-time work. Arrange for someone at home or a friend or a message service to take such calls, then check with them regularly and return all calls promptly. There is a good reason for this. You may feel at a psychological disadvantage if called while painting a neighbor's house or otherwise doing work beneath your educational level. Your professional manner will almost certainly suffer if you do. The exception, of course, is when you are engaged in part-time activities which are career-related. In that case, your stock will go up still higher with any prospective employer who learns you are already using the talents, skills, and education reflected in your resume.

YOU CAN INCREASE
YOUR QUALIFICATIONS

If finances permit, this is an ideal time to add to the education you have already acquired. A graduate-level course or two in your major will augment your undergraduate studies, while at the same time demonstrate your career seriousness to firms you will be contacting. Vocational or technical courses may offer specific training to underpin the theoretical knowledge you gained earlier.

As in the case of part-time work, continuing education offers a rich source of contacts for job referrals. Talk to the placement office, professors, and other students about the work you want to do. Follow up every lead.

HOW VOLUNTEER WORK
CAN ENHANCE YOUR CANDIDACY

There are many ways you can profit from doing volunteer work during this time. There is, of course, the personal satisfaction of having time to devote to favorite political, social, religious, or charity programs. Beyond that, however, is the benefit of meeting and mingling with people who many times turn out to be referrals to job opportunities. Most successful business people, government employees, and educators devote some of their time to volunteer work, and what better way to reach them than through an activity which has special significance to you both. Just be certain that your own enthusiasm for the particular volunteer organization has the ring of truth!

Our government's Office of Personnel Management, in its publication "Working For The USA," has this to say about volunteer work: "Unpaid experience or volunteer work in community, cultural, social service, or professional associations will count the same as paid experience, if it is of the type and level acceptable as paid experience for the job you want. When you are filling out your application forms, be sure to describe the work fully, showing the actual number of hours a week spent on the activity, in order to receive credit for it." Other employers could well have the same reaction.

DEVOTE SOME FREE TIME
TO YOURSELF

When planning the effective use of between-interview time, remember the *total* you. If urgent financial need dictates that you give first priority to paying, part-time work, be sure you plan other time for recreation, self-improvement, and social needs. Above all else, this uncertain period must not be allowed to develop a grim overtone. If it does, that grimness will rob you of enthusiasm and effectiveness in everything you set out to do. By recognizing that you do have personal needs and that they are important, you can achieve a balance that will serve you well.

YOUR JOB SEARCH
IS YOUR FIRST PRIORITY

In a sense, you must become a juggler of sorts during your job search, keeping your eye on all the free-time activities discussed and, at the same time, managing to keep that most important ball of all — your search for a full-time job — in the air at all times. You will want to maintain a steady, on-going relationship with your college placement office, of course. If too much time elapses between interviews they've arranged, exert a little pressure through personal visits or phone inquiries. Follow up, also, any contacts you make through part-time or volunteer work or continuing education. Be sure you scrutinize publications carrying help-wanted ads every day to stay abreast of openings or job possibilities.

It is essential, if you are to reach your goal in a reasonable amount of time, that you set up and maintain a schedule of just how you will spend your time. Decide how much you will devote per day and per week to each area of your between-interview activities. A good rule of thumb is to put job-search activities first and devote some part of every day to them. If you will be working three full days a week, plan to use lunch hours to read want ads or make phone calls lining up interviews. If your part-time work consists of a few hours every day, be sure some part of the remaining hours is set aside for research, interviews, phone calls, or following up personal contacts. The point is, keep track of how you spend your time and train yourself not to neglect any aspect of your job search.

After you have established a schedule, make periodic evaluations to see if you are actually accomplishing what you set out to do. You may find adjustments are called for, or it may be apparent that you are not getting as much done as you originally planned. Don't lower your expectations unless it is obvious you've set them too high. Instead, examine all the things you have done during the course of a week, determine why your progress is slower than you had expected, then make definite, detailed plans to make the changes called for.

Important advice: *Allow for mistakes.* Chances are there will be at least one interview experience you know you have mishandled, and if you replay that scene in your mind constantly, it may become a kind of jinx, leading to recurrence of your mistakes. The trick is to acknowledge what went wrong, decide how to correct it, then rehearse — alone or with a friend — an interview situation in which you handle things more successfully. You may make other mistakes, as well — push too hard with a personal contact, for instance, or so misrepresent your qualifications that you are instantly perceived as a "blowhard." It happens to almost every job applicant at one time or another, and the only remedy is to admit you blew it, and don't do it again! But agonizing over an error will do little other than add to your anxieties.

COPING WITH RELATIVES AND FRIENDS

One of the most sensitive aspects of the time between the start of your job search and employment is your relationships with those around you. Interactions with parents or guardians, friends, and professional acquaintances will almost certainly be affected by the course your job search is taking and the expectations they have for your speedy success. If your progress falls short of those expectations, you may fall prey to tensions, guilt, and estrangements.

Parents or guardians, especially, tend to look over their children's shoulders and direct their job-hunting efforts. They no doubt care a great deal about your happiness and they have, after all, probably provided or contributed to the cost of your college education. They have a vested interest in your becoming a wage earner who justifies their investment. They will be keenly interested in your before-graduation job-search activities and, if after graduation you still have not found a job and are living at home, you may represent an ongoing financial strain. Many times, grads in these circumstances develop such guilt complexes that they begin to avoid parents or guardians and a whole series of misunderstandings is set up which can result in long-lasting damage to emotional relationships.

The easiest way to prevent that damage is to maintain an open dialogue about your plans while you are looking for a job. Tell them which organizations you are concentrating on and why. Explain the process by which you hope to get interviews, and let them in on the results. In other words, communicate! If guilt feelings develop because you are still "living off them," talk to them about that, too — then either go to work part-time to pay a set room and board fee, or ask them to consider your support as a loan and agree on a definite weekly amount you will repay after you are employed. You will both feel better to get such feelings out in the open.

Your peers, too, will be watching your progress. Some will find jobs more quickly than you, others will still be unemployed after you have landed a position. Jealousy and backbiting are real dangers that can threaten friendships which have previously been solid. Here, again, communication is essential. Exchange interview experiences. Talk about upcoming interviews or prospects for future contacts. Make this a *shared* undertaking, and show an interest in your friends' plans, hopes, disappointments, and successes.

KEEP YOUR SPIRITS UP

What about your frame of mind during a job search that lasts longer than you had anticipated? *It is imperative that you not let your spirits lag!* Disappointment is a natural reaction to an interview that goes poorly, as well as to those long stretches of waiting to hear from others. But there is a simple way to combat its influence: recognize your disappointment, indulge it briefly, then *forget it and move on.* If you fail to do so, a feeling of inadequacy will begin to infect your attitude, a deadly consequence that can only lead to more disappointment.

Two very effective techniques in the struggle to keep your spirits high are 1) a system of rewards you give yourself, and 2) concentration on externals such as grooming and dress.

Rewards should be frequent and in recognition of personal victories. If you quake at the very thought of interviews, but have managed to get through several — regardless of their outcome — reward yourself in some way for your personal victory over those fears. You did, after all, get through the interviews. You deserve an afternoon off to squander at a favorite movie or in the park or on a new novel you've been wanting to read. When an interview goes particularly well, make your reward something really special. Celebrate your handling a feared situation in a satisfactory manner: perhaps buy the record or designer jeans you've wanted for a long time.

Each reward will shore up positive feelings about yourself, and the attitude employers see will be one of increasing self-confidence.

As for grooming and dress, make this a conscious part of your job search. Nothing so lifts the spirits as the feeling that you look good. Just going through the motions of getting a haircut or shining shoes or having clothing pressed can have a positive effect on your outlook. If you know you are dressed appropriately and are well groomed, your step will be jauntier and your tone of voice firmer.

IN BRIEF

From reading this chapter, you have learned how to use between-interview time productively by not letting up on your first priority — your job search; making your idle time pay off through part-time work with flexible hours; using this time to increase your educational background and technical skills; using volunteer work to satisfy personal desires while developing valuable job contacts; planning for needed recreational and social outlets; keeping your relatives and friends in touch with what you are doing, thus maintaining healthy personal relationships; and last, but certainly not least, keeping your own spirits high.

11

Recognizing
a Genuine
Job Offer

The interview went well, you established warm rapport with your interviewer, and you left feeling a job offer had been made. But, had it? And, if it really was an offer, is it the kind to which you should give serious consideration?

One of the most disillusioning experiences of job applicants is the letdown which follows what appears to be a firm commitment, but which turns out to be somewhat less than that. Interviewing techniques followed by some recruiters leave vague — or even misleading — impressions. Very seldom is this done intentionally. However, before you start out on a round of interviews, you should be armed with knowledge of some of the most common of these. More important, you should be able to recognize the elements that comprise a genuine job offer.

WHEN AN "OFFER"
IS NOT AN OFFER

A certain amount of misunderstanding arises when an over-anxious applicant misinterprets what is no more than "feeling out" activity on the part of the prospective employer. For example, you may interpret the question "Would you be willing to work irregular hours and be on call over weekends?" as *"Will* you be willing. . . ." and feel that your agreement to such terms means the job is yours. Never let yourself construe things in this way. Elementary, perhaps, but a mistake made by more than a few job hunters.

In the same vein, a general statement such as "Well, I think we have a meeting of minds here. Why don't you come back on Monday morning?" may *sound* like a job offer, but don't do any celebrating until Monday morning rolls around and that "meeting of the minds" is spelled out in detail.

Beware, too, of "We'll almost certainly be able to use you two months from now." If the job is one you really want, with the organization you most want to join, you may justifiably feel it is worth waiting for. After all, two months is not *too* long, and you might not find anything else, anyway. That's all fine and good IF this is a bona fide offer. But "almost certainly" and "two months from now" is vague. Do you have a firm offer? What will be your actual report-for-work date? Has a definite salary been established? Have job responsibilities been explained in detail? And, finally, do you know why the job will not be available immediately? In other words, you must determine if the interviewer is saying the job is yours in two months, or if this is a variation of "Check with us later, something may develop."

THE DANGER OF MISINTERPRETING "OFFERS"

Suppose you have had one or more interviews which ended with none of the indefinite "offers" described. You are not actually on a payroll yet, but you are as sure as you can be that a firm job commitment has been or will soon be made. Is your job search over? *It is not.* One of the most common mistakes job seekers make is to prematurely relax or stop their search. In the light of stark reality, *your job search is not over until you report for work!* Even if you have had signals that you are being favorably considered, developments you can neither foresee nor control may change the picture before you are hired.

Keep in mind always that you are presently engaged in what is really an extension of your career preparation. This is the final transition period from college to the workworld, and it calls for the best judgment and truest perception of the hiring process you can develop. Any misinterpretation on your part of an "offer" can distort perception, so be aware of the possibility of misunderstanding and concentrate on recognizing a real offer when it comes along.

ELEMENTS OF A GENUINE JOB OFFER

A firm job offer may be made verbally — usually after a series of interviews — or may come in written form. However the offer is made, it will contain (or, at least, it should contain) most or all of the following specific information:

- A clear "we are offering you the job" statement
- Your position title and a definition of duties
- Identification of your immediate supervisor
- Starting salary
- A description of conditions of employment such as probation period, initial training program, employee benefits, travel required, and so on
- The date and time to report for work

Not all employers make it a practice to mail written job-offer confirmations. There is nothing wrong with your asking for one at the time you get a verbal offer, but do not be surprised or alarmed if your future employer declines to do so. A useful step at that point would be for you to verbally review the items listed above, jotting down your own notes in case you need to refer to them later. Or, you might even take the initiative by sending a confirming acceptance letter to the employer, including the employment terms. Presumably, if there is any disagreement about terms, the employer will quickly respond.

Salary and certain other job aspects are possible subjects for negotiation at the time a firm offer is made. They'll be discussed in the next chapter.

IN BRIEF

To avoid disappointment and unnecessary delays in finding a job, you must learn to recognize genuine job offers by being aware of "feeling out" interview techniques which can sound like a firm offer; looking for key elements of a true offer such as when and where to report for work, introduction to your supervisor, and essential conditions of employment; and remembering that your job search is not over until you have unequivocal conformation that verifies your hire.

At this point, your attention turns to negotiating the best deal you can for yourself. That brings us to Chapter 12.

12

Negotiating
the Best Deal
For Yourself

Once you have received a firm offer of employment, you must decide if it is an acceptable one. A positive answer may depend on how well you negotiate its terms with your potential employer.

Unless the original offer is satisfactory to you in every respect, you will need to know: which factors are usually negotiable and which are not; your own minimum requirements for acceptance of the offer, that is, your negotiating base; and when and how to proceed with negotiations to get the best deal possible.

Beginning salary is the one item most likely to be open for negotiation when a job offer is made. While some organizations are tied to fixed starting salaries (and you will have to decide if you should "take it or leave it"), most have a salary range for hiring new employees.

If you know what the range is you will be in a much better position to negotiate. So your first step is to ask your potential employer about the range offered. If you are not given that information, there may be ways to arrive at a reasonable estimate which comes close to the actual figures. For one thing, check your placement office, frequently a reliable source for such data. If they are unable to help you, peruse help-wanted ads and ask fellow students about the ranges their prospective employers are offering. Often, within an industry, or among competing firms, salaries are quite similar, giving you better information than if you have to guess.

Generally, where a range exists there is room for discretion on the part of the person with whom you discuss starting salary. A normally effective strategy is to present your desired salary as a range — one that extends from the midpoint to above the top of the employer's range. For example, if you know that the starting salary range is $10,000 to $14,000, and you are asked for the salary you desire, say that you hope to start in the $12,000 to $15,000 area. Doing so may help you get an offer near the high side of the range.

The job market, itself, will determine to a large extent an employer's willingness to alter the salary originally offered. If your field is one of high demand and low supply, you obviously begin every interview from a strong negotiating point. Even in an overcrowded labor market, if your qualifications go beyond the norm — if you have unusual expertise in a special phase of the work or advanced study or extensive practical experience — beginning salary might be negotiable.

Geographic location can play a part, as in the case of employees who were paid higher for work on the Alaskan pipe line than the scale normally paid for similar work, or special salary arrangements or cost of living bonuses for employees willing to work out of the country.

"Time" elements are other negotiating possibilities: a delayed starting date, specific vacation dates, leaving early to take a course, or an extended holiday weekend if you have prior commitments and make those plans known to the employer. This applies, of course, to those upcoming near the time you are asked to report for work. Rarely will any organization make *permanent* concessions of this sort for an entry-level employee (although the author knows of one engineer, starting to work for a small manufacturer, who was able to negotiate St. Patrick's Day as an annual personal holiday!)

Factors usually not subject to negotiation are: **fringe benefits** (type of coverage, amount of employee contribution, and so on); amount of **vacation time** (although specific dates, or taking some vacation time before satisfying a minimum length of service requirement can sometimes be arranged); **work hours** (if the employer has "flex-time," limited negotiation may be possible); and **rules and regulations** which are a matter of policy (such as dress code, smoking restrictions or standards of performance).

YOUR NEGOTIATING BASE FOR SALARY

How can you determine what salary to shoot for? Well, to begin with, you must know how much any job *must* pay you to be acceptable. Let's look at the calculations that will go into that determination.

To set a minimum figure you must earn, you will have to have a realistic picture of just what your living expenses will be. Sit down and list in writing everything you will be responsible for paying (Figure 12.1 will help you do so). It may be necessary to estimate some of these expenses; housing costs, for example, if you are now living at home but plan to move out once you are employed. But all estimates should be based on carefully researched knowledge of what you can reasonably expect them to be in your potential employer's locality. That means going beyond the reports of friends or acquaintances to get the hard facts. Read ads which give clues to living costs (rental, grocery, clothing, and so on) until you have a pretty good idea of what each item is going to cost you. Now, total all your current bill payments (will you be repaying college loans? personal loans? buying a car?). If you will be setting up your own household, find out what you can expect utility bills to be and add those figures to your list. If funds for savings or investment represent a basic necessity to you, add them in. Do not forget that personal needs must be included in any assessment of total needs.

There is yet another step in calculating your negotiating base: allowing for legal deductions which will be made from earnings. Federal deductions have to be determined. Where applicable, state and city income taxes must be taken into account. There may be employee contributory insurance premiums to be deducted. These cannot be accurately projected before a specific job offer is made, but should be provided for on an estimated basis. (Your placement office, personnel or payroll departments of potential employers, and personal contacts are sources of information for your estimates.)

Figure 12.1 is a listing which covers all these requirements, plus some others of equal importance. If the object of work was only to earn enough to meet *basic* needs, then "employment" would have grim overtones, indeed! While it may not be essential for mere sur-

```
┌─────────────────────────────────────────────────────────────┐
│                                                               │
│        BUDGET WORKSHEET FOR RECENT COLLEGE GRADUATE           │
│                                                               │
│     Food and beverages                      $_____        │
│                                                               │
│     Clothing and upkeep                      _____        │
│                                                               │
│     Housing, utilities, furnishings          _____        │
│                                                               │
│     Medical care                             _____        │
│                                                               │
│     Transportation (exluding auto loan)      _____        │
│                                                               │
│     Personal (health & beauty aids)          _____        │
│                                                               │
│     Continuing education                     _____        │
│                                                               │
│     Recreation                               _____        │
│                                                               │
│     Savings                                  _____        │
│                                                               │
│     Insurance (personal, auto, household)    _____        │
│                                                               │
│     Contributions and gifts                  _____        │
│                                                               │
│     Dues                                     _____        │
│                                                               │
│     Debts (loans and interest repayment)     _____        │
│                                                               │
│     Taxes                                    =========        │
│                                                               │
│            TOTAL                            $_____        │
│                                                               │
│                                                               │
└─────────────────────────────────────────────────────────────┘
```

FIGURE 12.1

vival, a *discretionary* income is a necessity in a very real sense. Depending on your personal priorities for each, continuing education, recreation, cultural pursuits, saving, and perhaps a few luxuries, should be included in your calculations to negotiate a base figure. Certainly this is not an easy task; your initial impulse is likely to be a quick "the more the better," when it comes to setting a required figure for discretionary income. But when looking for that all-important entry-level job, the figure for discretionary income is one of your most valuable tools in the salary negotiating process, and the flexibility it may require.

Discretionary income is the one area that allows you to weigh the advantages of a job which pays less initially, but offers sound career growth potential, against one with a higher beginning salary, but limited promotion possibilities. If you have the foresight to recognize those advantages and can successfully put a higher discretionary income "on hold" for the time being, you will be able to make a temporary sacrifice in favor of long-term gains. In effect, this is where you can *negotiate with yourself* when considering job offers.

> Don't turn down a good opportunity because the starting salary is too low. Regard it as an investment in your future.
>
> DR. CAROL FINN MEYER
> VICE PRESIDENT
> CROSSLEY SURVEYS

Of course, you will not necessarily be faced with such a choice. Some newly hired employees are fortunate enough to have both strong career opportunity and gratifying income. But sometimes hard choices have to be made, and when that's the case, consider the advice of Dr. Bruce J. Walker, Professor of Marketing, College of Business Administration, Arizona State University: "Starting salary certainly should not be disregarded since it not only will determine your standard of living but also is an indicator of the value that the organization attaches to you. However, starting salary should be balanced against longer-term considerations. For instance, how much valuable knowledge and experience related to your chosen career field can be gained through the position? Does the position hold promise for future advancement that coincides with your career plans?"

That point of view is reinforced by Sid Bernstein, Chairman of the Executive Committee, Crain Communications: "Youthful job seekers looking for entry level positions should pay far more attention to trying to find a place doing the kind of work in which they are interested, and with the kind of organization they'd like to be associated with, than to how much money they are going to make."

If calculations for income must be somewhat flexible, how can you set a base negotiating figure? By establishing a realistic minimum and projecting a reasonable maximum, giving yourself a range within which to move. You must arrive at that minimum yourself; no one else can know your personal tolerance for postponing the pleasures to be purchased with available funds. As for the maximum, go to the marketplace. From college placement offices, want ads and personal contacts, you will be able to form a "going rate" assessment of salaries in your chosen field.

One excellent source of information is the College Placement Council starting salary surveys, conducted several times a year. Another highly useful source is the annual Endicott Report, published by the Placement Center of Northwestern University, which includes starting salary information for various fields in business and industry. Most placement offices receive one or both; sometimes they can be found in libraries or at employers' offices.

If the usual on-campus training is about all you have to offer, recognize that you will probably begin work at a salary in the lower register of the hiring range. If you have heavy work experience or exceptional involvement in career-related activities, you can raise your beginning salary expectations (and don't forget that some employers pay premiums for high grades, so take yours into account, if they are exceptional).

As you can see, a vital part of the negotiating process begins long before you enter an interviewer's office. Without this preparation, there is the possibility of letting glorified fringe benefits or future prospects blind you to a too-low beginning salary or conversely, to be beguiled by a higher-than-average salary in a dead-end job which will lead to personal and job dissatisfaction in the future.

An extremely useful method of weighing job offer alternatives is with factor analysis and a Decision/Analysis chart. This approach is clearly detailed in *The Job Game* by Ross Figgins (Prentice-Hall, 1980), and reproduced in this book as Appendix E.

WHEN YOU CAN NEGOTIATE

As a general rule, to be most effective, your negotiations should begin only after you have explored all the unchangeables of the job and have had at least one opportunity (preferably several in a series of interviews) to sell yourself and your value to the interviewing organization. Any sooner, and your position may be weakened for no other reason than the fact that the employer is not fully aware of your special abilities and all the qualifications which increase your market value. Sometimes the subject is raised for you, when the employer expresses interest in hiring you and asks what starting salary you are looking for. If you raise the subject, be sure to do so only when you feel reasonably certain that the employer is about to make you a job offer, or has already done so.

HOW YOU CAN NEGOTIATE

In the negotiating process, there is one very important intangible which many times helps determine the outcome: *your own self-confidence.* Remember, no matter what career you are headed for, at this moment *you are in sales.* If your belief in your *you* product is reflected in your manner, dress, and speech, the price for that product is much more likely to satisfy you.

At the time you are quoted a beginning salary figure, you will have to decide whether it satisfies your anticipated budget. Your desire should be realistic in terms of salaries normally paid to those starting in similar positions with employers in similar fields.

For example, an employer might say: "We'd like to have you join us at $11,000 a year." If that offer permits you to meet your expected financial needs, determined by your expense estimates, you may well decide to accept the offer and not even consider negotiating. But if the salary offered for a desirable job is short of your expectations, you might decide to try to boost the offer. This is best done by expressing a bit of hesitancy while reminding the employer of your formal education, applicable work experience, leadership qualities, competitive offers you have already received, or any other strong points which might open the door to an upward adjustment.

Even if you wind up with the salary originally quoted, the person responsible for hiring will be keenly aware of your confidence in your own ability and the value you place on yourself.

Be careful not to overdo that confidence, however, if you know this is the job you want and if you are satisfied that the salary offered is a fair one within the range you know to be realistic, albeit a little lower than you would like. Remember, you are negotiating, *not* issuing an ultimatum. In other words, don't negotiate yourself out of a job you really want. Consider, too, the frequency of performance appraisals which could lead to promotions and higher pay. You may be able to live with a lower-than-expected beginning salary if there is the prospect of advancement in, say, six months.

What to do if the offer is a flat, "We start all people in your position at $9,000 a year"? Even if that figure is below the absolute minimum you have determined as acceptable, *ask* about the possibility of negotiating before you turn it down if most or all other factors are favorable. A simple, "Is the beginning salary negotiable in the light of my special qualifications?" may re-open the matter of money. Or, if you feel the interviewer has been impressed with your application, you might ask if it is possible to reclassify the job so that it falls into another salary range. This could be a negotiating route which may have been overlooked by the interviewer.

Should the initially offered figure prove to be a firm one, you have at least asked, leaving an impression of self-confidence. If you must decline the offer at that salary, the person doing the hiring is much more likely to keep you in mind for future, higher-paying openings.

Negotiations for things other than salary should also be entered into when the offer is made. Ask for concessions in a pleasant, conversational tone and decide in advance whether they are important enough to warrant declining the offer if they are denied.

IN BRIEF

In order to negotiate the most favorable terms of employment for your entry-level job, you should be aware of negotiable factors, as well as those which cannot be negotiated; determine what you must earn to meet basic living expenses and to provide sufficient discretionary income for personal needs, both of which will enable you to arrive at an acceptable salary range within which to negotiate, using current job market conditions to set the range maximum; leave most negotiating until after you are fully familiar with all conditions and demands of the job; know and express confidence in any special qualifications such as past achievements, education, experience, or personal qualities which increase your value in the job market. Remember to sell yourself!

13

Getting Off to a Good Start on the New Job

YOU'RE HIRED! What a glorious feeling. In truth, a host of feelings: elation, satisfaction, and most of all, relief that your entry-level job search has ended.

Relax and enjoy your well-deserved emotions — you've earned them. But recognize, too, that while your "job of finding a job" is over, your career is just beginning. *How* you start your new job can make a world of difference in the degree of success and self-fulfillment it brings you. From the moment you accept a job offer, there are things you can do to make that start a good one.

BEFORE YOU REPORT TO WORK

How you accept the offer is an important part of getting off on the right foot. Do it *enthusiastically*. Let your new boss know how happy you are to be joining the organization, and do it in writing. If the offer has been made in a personal interview or by phone, you may want to ask for a confirmation letter setting out the major terms of employment and exactly when and where you are to report the first day.

Remember all those other interviews? Any for which your application is still under consideration should be contacted with a short note explaining that you have accepted employment elsewhere. Be sure to thank them for the time and consideration already given you. Why? Good manners, first of all. But even more important, those interviews are *contacts* you have made in your field of interest, and they may well prove valuable in the future.

It's possible you will have some further dealings with them even while in the job you have accepted, and if you have maintained good relations, they will stand you in good stead. Furthermore, if the job you are taking doesn't work out — for whatever reason — you will be able to reapply with the assurance that the impression you previously made was positive.

There are other personal details which should be attended to before you report for work. Be sure your clothes are in order so you won't be faced with last-minute dry cleaning or small purchases to complete your working wardrobe. Free your time of outstanding personal commitments such as medical or dental appointments. If you will be using your car to get to work, be sure it's in good working order. Your own condition is important, too; if job-search activities or part-time work have left you more than a little fatigued, now is the time to take a few days off to recharge your batteries so you will arrive on that momentous first day refreshed and ready to demonstrate your best performance.

YOUR FIRST DAY

Your first day on the job should begin with your showing up just a bit ahead of time. Five or ten minutes before starting time is fine.

By and large, your first day at work will most likely be taken up by a carefully planned schedule. Probably some orientation, formal or informal to acquaint you more fully with procedures, policies, and regulations, as well as introductory rounds in your neighboring departments. You may be asked to lunch with your new co-workers, or even your boss. Whatever the routine set out for you, unless you are super-human, that first day will be a nerve-wracking one. You will feel you are on display, as indeed you are. Awkward as that may make you feel, hang on to your basic good business manners, do the very best you can, and remember that many of those you meet will feel that they, too, are being observed *by you.* If the day ends with nothing but a hazy memory of a million details and faces and names and places you know you should remember, but cannot — relax. This is, after all, your first day; no one is going to expect you to absorb everything at once, and tomorrow things will begin to sort themselves out. Procedures will become familiar once you have followed them; names and faces will assume personalities you will remember.

One personnel director describes the orientation process in these terms: "When you get your first paycheck, you wonder whether you've earned it — everything is so new to you, you don't feel you're making much of a contribution. When your second paycheck arrives, you've started to get the hang of things, and feel it's fair recompense for what you've been doing. And by the time you get your third paycheck, you're well enough enmeshed and productive to start wondering when you'll be getting your first salary increase!"

SETTLING IN

There are a few simple rules of business etiquette that bear repeating, since your observance of them will strike the right note with co-workers and supervisors alike.

Telephone Courtesy

In most positions, the telephone plays a key role. How you use it is important. Always answer by identifying yourself by name (and department, if that is the practice — observe co-workers and follow their lead). When calling others, leave a message or call-back if they are tied up. Never have them called out of a meeting except for matters of extreme urgency. Bring your conversation to an end as soon as your purpose has been accomplished, but do it pleasantly and cordially, not abruptly. Return business calls as soon as you possibly can.

If you must ask someone to hold the line, make their wait as brief as possible. Get the required information or attend to the interruption quickly. If a long wait will be involved, ask if you may call back to continue the conversation.

Moderate your telephone voice so that it does not disturb others in the immediate vicinity. Confidential or sensitive matters are normally not appropriate for the telephone. Ask for an appointment to discuss them in a private setting.

Personal calls which must be made or accepted at the office

(and everyone has them from time to time) should be brief. If they require more time, try to call back during lunch or a break period.

Meetings with Your Supervisor

In the beginning, you will probably spend a good deal of time with your supervisor. Afterwards, when you are working more on your own, there will be times you need a private session. When those occasions arise, be sure you observe office protocol; make an appointment through a secretary if that is the practice. If not, make a direct request either in person or by phone, and give your supervisor an idea of the amount of time you will need. Watch your timing; heavy pressure days are *not* the time to ask for a conference on something that can wait for a less hectic time.

Never just barge into your supervisor's office, no matter how important you believe your need for a conference. If your request for a private meeting is based on emotional stress, cool it overnight. It is amazing how your perspective can change after a good night's rest!

Getting Along with Co-Workers

Your co-workers are an important part of your new environment. You will need their cooperation and their acceptance, so give top priority to cultivating good office relationships. You do that primarily by observing the rules of common courtesy and consideration that apply in all other phases of your life. There is one big difference, however, where fellow employees are concerned. While you can choose your personal friends, you usually have no voice in selecting those with whom you must work. That means you have to work that much harder to get along with them all, not just your favorites. Without the cooperation of people who work together on a civilized basis, the job cannot be done smoothly — and *that* should be your objective.

Tactfulness

Tact is your most useful tool in dealing with co-workers. Think about the requests you must make of others — help in locating files, important information or equipment — and practice phrasing them in a tactful manner. Consider, for example, the difference in another person's response to "Get me the Smith Company file. I need it in a hurry," and, "Harry, I'm in a rush to get the Smith Company file in to Mr. X. Would you do me a favor and get it for me, please?" The first will engender resentment; the latter, cooperation. After the first few days on the job, you will be able to anticipate some of the situations most likely to come up when you will have to make such requests and you can think ahead about your manner. However, the best possible approach is to make tact a natural part of your dealings with others so that whatever you are asking, recommending, or correcting, it will be done in a friendly, non-offensive way.

Careful Listening

Especially in the beginning days and weeks, your relations with other workers will depend a great deal on how well you *listen.* If you are to avoid the deadly "college grad know-it-all" tag, you must not only ask questions in a courteous manner, but learn to listen carefully to answers. Listen, too, to tips passed along by friendly fellow employees. You are not obliged to follow their judgment on the best way to do things or get along in the company (indeed, *you* must form your own opinions and guidelines for *your* behavior), but do give them the courtesy of an attentive audience.

"Listen," with your eyes as well. Watch what goes on between co-workers, supervisors, management, and clients. Absorb as much as you can about the way things are done. You may well feel they need improvement and you may have solutions. This, however, is not the time to present them. Right now, you are building a base of good relationships from which you can later make suggestions for improvement. And, although you may not think it at the moment, time may reveal underlying reasons for procedures that are unknown to you at this point. Your job now, therefore, is to listen, watch, and learn.

> Impatience is at once the greatest asset and the greatest liability of youth. It is an asset because impatience makes people strive to better themselves, their profession, and their community. Impatience is a liability when it leads young people to try to start at the top, or very close to it. My advice is to aim high, but be willing to start at the very bottom.
>
> CECIL D. ANDRUS
> SECRETARY OF THE INTERIOR
> UNDER PRESIDENT JIMMY CARTER

Marie J. De Stena, career counselor at Fordham University's Career Counseling and Placement Center, offers this very useful advice: "Look for positive role models. For example, you may find an experienced worker or a supervisor you wish to emulate. Assess and identify their personal qualities, career skills, work orientation, and the paths they took in the company to attain their positions. Many times a relationship will develop with such a person who then becomes a mentor. It will be fortunate for you if this happens in that it is important to have models and mentors in your beginning jobs."

Here is some helpful counsel from Elmer B. Staats, retired Comptroller General of the United States: "Commit yourself to a program of continuing education and personal development. One of the greatest shortcomings which I find in individual progress is the failure to recognize the need to keep up to date in professional and technical fields. Participating in professional organizations, in particular, can play an important part in personal self-development."

Office Politics

In almost every organization, there is a certain amount of politicking — workers and supervisors alike jockeying for position in the power structure. It is important, especially in the beginning, that you stay out of those situations and not unwittingly become a pawn in someone else's strategy. It can be tricky. As a new employee, you may not be aware of dangerous undercurrents. Your best bet is to listen to what everyone has to say, avoid taking a definite stand on issues which are new to you, and concentrate on doing your own job well. Later on, you may become a vital part of just such in-company maneuvering. But jumping into the fray during your breaking-in period is *not* the way to get off to a good start.

Positive Thinking

Another danger for newly hired employees is that of catching the "anti-employer infection" from veteran employees who have a negative view of their own work, the organization, and probably themselves. Unfortunately, it is a rare organization that is completely free of these gloomy employees. Your best defense is to express understanding for their feelings and remember that every job and every company has some shortcomings. There are dull, repetitious chores in the most exciting of vocations; unpleasant and incompetent workers in the best of organizations. To maintain your own positive attitude, go back to all that pre-employment research and review the things that attracted you to the employer in the first place. Keep your eye on those aspects and leave the backbiting to others. Do not, however, come on so strong with your enthusiasm about the organization or your job that you come across as a starry-eyed rookie. Hold all those cheers in check during work hours. Temper them with reality as time goes by, and indulge them all you want away from your workplace.

Social Contacts

What about socializing with co-workers? In a sense you will be doing that all day, every day. No one wants to work with a "strictly business" personality. A pleasant greeting, amiable chats off and on during the day, and genuine interest in others as people (not simply cogs in the work world's wheel) are the ingredients for sound, healthy work relationships. Should you extend that socializing beyond work hours? Perhaps. There are, of course, organization-sponsored social activities which are designed to reinforce good relations. You will undoubtedly want to see some of your co-workers on your own during nonwork hours, and to deny yourself that pleasure would be foolish. The cardinal rule, however, is to draw a firm line between your personal life and your work life — and do not cross it! The overlapping of personal and business activities has scuttled more than one promising career, so keep a tight grip on a perspective that values each separate from the other.

A Rose Is a Rose . . .

How do you address your superiors? The answer varies with different employers. Whether it will be "Jim" or "Mr. Smith," "Sally" or "Miss Jones" depends on the employer's traditions. Your clues will quickly come from those around you — fellow employees with similar positions. But until you learn your organization's practices, avoid first names until they are suggested to you. If you are not sure what to do, there is a good Army rule to follow: "If it moves, salute it."

Give It Your Best Shot

Finally, while an awareness of all these precepts can help steer you through those first days and weeks, your acceptance by co-workers will be *most* influenced by *how you do your job*. That does not mean that you must always be letter-perfect. Everyone makes mistakes. Admit yours gracefully, ask for help or advice, and you will win the support of fellow employees as well as supervisors. Pull your weight in a friendly, cooperative spirit, and you will earn their respect, a vital element in any long-lasting relationship. If you drag your feet, or project an arrogant I-don't-need-you attitude, you will find the workworld a cold, lonely place. "There is no substitute for hard work and determination," says U.S. Senator Daniel Patrick Moynihan (New York). "One's greatest reward can come from a job well done." That essential ingredient for success was echoed by A. W. Clausen, president of the World Bank, when he was president and chief executive officer of BankAmerica Corporation: "Don't think that because you're just out of school or just promoted into official

ADJUSTMENT PROBLEMS OF NEWLY-EMPLOYED COLLEGE GRADUATES*

Respondents were asked to indicate the most difficult problems which new college graduates face in adjusting to employment in business. A total of 165 companies responded.

Major adjustment problems are listed below in order of frequency of mention:

Number
of Companies

66 Transition from classroom learning to job experience. Relating theory to practical situations.

43 Adjusting to the routine aspects of the job, regular hours, and scheduled assignments.

35 Understanding how business operates. Adjusting to the corporate structure and business environment.

33 Adjusting expectations to reality. Expecting too much too soon. Setting realistic goals.

25 Learning to work effectively with many types of people. Personal relations, developing a cooperative attitude toward supervisors and other workers, many of whom are older.

20 Accepting responsibility and getting the job done. Determining what is most important in making decisions.

16 Understanding the philosophy of management in a profit-oriented organization. Understanding what motivates executives.

14 Re-examining interests, abilities and values. Recognizing inadequacies. Finding themselves.

11 Adjusting to a new location. Living in a different community.

10 Learning to communicate effectively. Overcoming inadequate writing skills.

*SOURCE: The Endicott Report, 1977. Published and copyrighted by The Placement Center, Northwestern University, Evanston, Illinois.

ranks, it's all over—that you've got it made. There's still a lot to learn. And to the extent that you're willing to put in the time and effort and make sacrifices, the rewards will be proportionate. If your performance is truly outstanding, then you will get truly outstanding recognition. If your performance is average, you'll get average recognition."*

*With permission from MBA Executive.

WHAT DOES YOUR SUPERVISOR
THINK OF YOU?

Most large organizations in business, education, and government, have formal appraisal programs. They provide an opportunity for an employee to learn about how his or her supervisor perceives performance and personality. To be effective, such appraisals should be constructive and forward-looking, emphasizing development, growth, and advancement.

If you are working for an employer who has a formal system, you are likely to be made aware of it early in your career — certainly during your first year of employment.

If there is no formal appraisal system, give serious consideration to initiating your own "appraisal review" with your supervisor, so that you do not lose out on the benefits which can come from appraisal by your superior. Here are questions which can guide both you and your supervisor in assessing your performance and structuring a plan for your development:

1. Job Knowledge. Know job well? Aware of company facilities for performance of job and solutions of problems? Have sufficient knowledge of products/services, operations, organization, competition? Keep abreast of new trends and developments in field of activity?

2. Work Quality. Successfully direct energies toward total scope of assignment, rather than only dealing with individual parts? Does work performed usually satisfy the needs identified? Is work planned and organized?

3. Work Quantity. Are volume requirements of job complied with?

4. Writing Skills. Are written communications clear and concise? If writing for public, is work imaginative, tasteful, on target with goals?

5. Oral Skills. Able to verbally express ideas, defend position, present effectively? Exude confidence and persuasiveness? Field questions well?

6. Inside Contacts. Deal harmoniously and productively with fellow employees? Maintain good relationships with superiors and subordinates? Tactful, considerate, cooperative with others?

7. Outside Contacts. Effectively handle dealings with people outside (clients, suppliers, and so on)? Have their respect? Able to develop a base of influential and informative contacts?

8. Involvement. High degree of commitment? Perform beyond mere response to requests or requirements? Make the effort to know and understand the organization's goals beyond normal routines?

9. Responsibility. Accept responsibility for own or subordinate's work? Admit when wrong?

10. Dependability and Determination. Complete assignments on time? Organize and follow through on appropriate courses of action? Need little or no supervision?

11. Initiative and Resourcefulness. Recognize, on own, what has to be done and then do it? Adapt quickly to sudden changes or priority shifts? Set priorities for self? Go beyond the mere requirements of an assignment?

12. Versatility. Work successfully on a problem for which has had little or no previous experience? Translate different experiences to the solving of problems at hand?

13. Creativity and Originality. Develop fresh and original ideas, practices, methods?

14. Decisiveness. Have the courage and ability to identify what believes to be the best answer, and then defend position?

15. Judgment. Weigh all important factors before arriving at a decision? Analyze a situation and develop meaningful and practical ideas and solutions?

16. Leadership. Inspire confidence and respect? Effective in group interaction? Delegate responsibility when appropriate to do so? Recognize the need to develop and promote capable subordinates?

17. Cost Consciousness and Control. Careful to avoid waste? Take steps to reduce labor and material costs?

18. Maturity. Able to take criticism? Exhibit sound emotional balance under stress? Anticipate problems and help avoid crises? Properly maintain confidences?

19. Attitude. Interested in work? Seek opportunities to make contributions to organization efforts? Positivistic? Enthusiastic? Display pride in job and the organization?

20. Personal Appearance and Habits. Is appearance generally appropriate for position? Are there any habits which may affect ability to handle job or cause irritation to others?

21. What are the appraisee's strong points?

22. What are the appraisee's limitations?

23. What, specifically, can be done by (a) the appraisee and (b) the supervisor to help the appraisee develop full capacity in present position? When will steps be taken? (Consider: training, change of duties, additional responsibilities, special counseling, additional schooling, and similar developmental actions).

FINAL WORD

Success in finding and keeping a desirable job is directly tied to the degree of effort you apply. In the world of work, the elusive factor of "luck" inevitably favors the well-prepared!

Afterword

Advice from many "idea contributors" has been included throughout this book with the belief that we all need heroes, and we tend to be responsive to those who are "in the know." This is especially true for those who are inexperienced in the workworld, venturing out on their first full-time jobs.

As a fitting conclusion to this book, seven thoughtful and helpful quotes appear below. Reflection on each will provide you with additional insights into career decision-making, the job-seeking process, and on-the-job performance.

> Don't be concerned if upon graduation you have little understanding of your own talents or focus on your life's work. Only a minority are given such insights in their early years. Most have to find their way by diverse job experiences.
>
> FRANK SHAKESPEARE, PRESIDENT
> R K O GENERAL

To be successful, one must be able effectively to manage time — the only non-renewable, non-replaceable resource. Successful time management

must be on two levels. The first and most obvious is day-by-day management, which has been the subject of many excellent books. The more
critical factor of time management has not been dealt with as extensively.
It is that if certain decisions are not made by a given point in time, the
options have been forfeited. For example, a decision to become a ranked
professional tennis player must be made in one's teen years, if not sooner.
Similarly, in many professions and careers, decisions must be made early
—generally no later than in one's 20's or early 30's—or the option may
not exist.

ALBERT P. HEGYI, PRESIDENT
ASSOCIATION OF MBA EXECUTIVES INC.

Career-minded college graduates should be flexible in considering employment that might be offered to them. The opportunities available
to men and women entering the job market are often increased significantly if the applicants approach their initial starting position with an
open mind.

WALTER S. HOLMES, JR.
CHAIRMAN OF THE BOARD
C.I.T. FINANCIAL CORPORATION

Don't be afraid to take a risk. If you are not certain about the exact kind
of job you want, after some extended reflection, jump into the fray
nevertheless. There are many things one can learn about one's capabilities
and one's psychological needs and interests through the very experience
of working. The important point here is, don't be afraid to experiment.
But when the message of the experiment is —I am not growing—I am not
being enriched—I am not enjoying ... then, before you get too en-
trenched in material fruits of working—change—until you find that
position that will make you richer as a person as well as richer as
a consumer.

DAVID L. SHANNON
DIRECTOR OF PERSONNEL
BOARD OF GOVERNORS OF THE FEDERAL RESERVE SYSTEM

Here are some questions that an individual might review from time to
time in assessing career development:
a. How have I applied myself to tasks at hand? What methods have I
used to achieve results? How was I most successful in presenting my
ideas?
b. What assignments that required an evaluation by a teacher, manager, or
chief executive did I enjoy doing the most? Preparing independent
projects? Managing groups? Initiating programs? Selling items or ideas?
Negotiating? Collecting data? Communicating information?

DONALD C. CARROLL, DEAN
THE WHARTON SCHOOL
UNIVERSITY OF PENNSYLVANIA

After you have been with your new employer for three to six months, map out a career plan you would like to see develop. Promise yourself to reevaluate your career at least annually.

DENNIS B. SULLIVAN, PRESIDENT
VLASIC FOODS, INC.

Life moves at a faster pace as years go by, and when the milestones of promotions or career-advancing job changes are past, time spent at apprenticeship seems short, indeed. The more cheerfully one can undertake that period, the shorter it is apt to be.

JAMES F. CALVANO
PRESIDENT AND CHIEF EXECUTIVE OFFICER
AVIS, INC.

Appendices

Appendix A:
Sources of Information
on Internships and Summer Jobs

INTERNSHIPS

Student Guide to Internships, National Society for Internships and Experiential Education, 1735 I Street, Suite 601, Washington, D.C. 20006.

Directory of Undergraduate Internships, source same as above.

Directory of Washington Internships, source same as above.

Directory of Public Service Internships: Opportunities for the

Graduate, Post-Graduate and Mid-Career Professional, source same as above.

Internship Programs for Women, source same as above.

Storming Washington: An Intern's Guide to National Government, Political Science Association, 1527 New Hampshire Avenue, NW, Washington, D.C. 20036.

The International Directory for Youth Internships, U.N. Headquarters NGO Youth Courses, c/o Center for Social Development and Humanitarian Affairs, Room DC-976, United Nations, New York, NY 10017.

International Directory of Youth Internships: A Directory of Intern Volunteer Opportunities, Foreign Area Materials Center, Suite 1231, 60 East 42nd Street, New York, NY 10017.

Directory of Internships, Work Experience Programs and On-the-Job Training Opportunities, Ready Reference Press, P.O. Box 5169, Santa Monica, CA 90405.

Invest Yourself, Commission on Voluntary Service Action, 475 Riverside Drive, Room 1700A, New York, NY 10027.

The Student Guide to Mass Media Internships, Research Group, Box 52, Regent Hall, University of Colorado, Boulder, CO 80309.

Professional societies are often aware of opportunities for internships in the field of a student's choice. The *Occupational Outlook Handbook,* available in most career counseling offices, university, college, and public libraries, cites organizations which represent the interests of most professions and occupations. The student interested in a particular field can address a request to the appropriate organization and ask for information on internships.

SUMMER JOBS

19xx Summer Employment Directory of the U.S., Writer's Digest, 9933 Alliance Road, Cincinnati, OH 45242 (annually).

19xx Directory of Overseas Summer Jobs, source same as above.

Summer Jobs in Britain, 19xx, source same as above.

Summer Jobs in Federal Agencies, U.S. Civil Service Commission, Washington, D.C. 20415.

Appendix B:
Useful Resources for Students
Seeking Jobs

Note: Most of these publications are updated periodically or, at the least, irregularly. Therefore, unless it is a book, publication dates or edition numbers are not included; your librarian can direct you to the most current copy on hand.

Ad Search. Milwaukee, WI: Ad Search, Inc., weekly. Employment openings available, culled from newspapers around the country, arranged by job title (Accounting to Technical). Also has Positions-Wanted section.

Advance Job Listings. New York: McGraw-Hill, weekly. Help-wanted advertisements compiled from 25 McGraw-Hill magazines, primarily edited for engineers, scientists, and technical managers.

Affirmative Action Register. Warren H. Green, Editor. St. Louis, MO: Affirmative Action Register, monthly. Help-wanted advertisements from employers throughout the nation. Provides female, minority, and handicapped candidates a chance to learn of professional, managerial, and administrative positions advertised by employers trying to satisfy their affirmative action goals.

Applied Science & Technology Index. New York: H. W. Wilson, monthly except July. Subject index to periodicals in the fields of aeronautics and space science, chemistry, computer technology and applications, construction industry, energy resources and research, engineering, fire and fire prevention, food and food industry, geology, machinery, mathematics, mineralogy, metallurgy, oceanography, petroleum and gas, physics, plastics, textile industry and fabrics, transportation, and other industrial and mechanical arts.

Association of MBA Executives. MBA Employment Guide. New York: Association of MBA Executives, annually. Although addressed to MBA's, this guide can be readily used by undergraduates as well. Over 1,000 employer entries are indexed by name, primary business function, and location. Contains several articles related to job search.

Ayer Directory of Publications. Bala Cynwyd, PA: Ayer Press, annually. An authoritative reference tool for current, accurate, and useful information relating to consumer, business, technical, professional, trade, and farm publications. Includes name, address, publication schedule, and cost of newspapers, magazines, and journals published in the U.S. and Engish-speaking environs.

Business Periodicals Index. Bettie Jane Third, ed. New York: H. W. Wilson, monthly except August. Articles related to companies and subject fields of interest to the job seeker. Articles describing companies are indexed under the name of the company. Subject fields include accounting, advertising and public relations, banking, building, chemicals, communications, computers, drugs and cosmetics, economics, electronics, finance and investments, industrial relations, insurance, international business, management and personnel administration, marketing, paper, petroleum, printing, real estate.

Career Guide to Professional Associations: A Directory of Organizations by Occupational Field. Cranston, RI: The Carroll Press. Provides name, mailing address, and types of career aids available from some 2,000 professional associations. Arranged according to the occupational classifications in the Dictionary of Occupational Titles, and has a cross index arranged alphabetically by career field, from accounting to writing.

Career Index. Moravia, NY: Chronicle Guidance Inc., annually. A reference listing of free or inexpensive vocational and educational guidance materials for counselors and students, from some 800 sources. Listed (and described) alphabetically by source and cross-referenced by occupational, professional, or educational subjects.

Career Information for College Graduates: An Annotated Bibliography. Eastern College Personnel Officers, Compiler, Bethlehem, PA: College Placement Council. Hundreds of references related to all aspects of career investigation.

College Placement Annual. Bethlehem, PA: College Placement Council, annually. Detailed occupational needs and contact information for over 1,300 employers who recruit college graduates. Articles on self-evaluation and job-seeking strategies.

Dictionary of Occupational Titles. Washington, D.C.: U.S. Department of Labor, Employment and Training Administration, 1977. Compendium of some 20,000 occupations. Integrated arrangement of occupational definitions and a classification structure to group them in terms of related duties and activities. Titles arranged alphabetically and by industry. Has sections on using the Dictionary as an occupational reference source and a glossary of defined technical terms.

Directory of American Firms Operating in Foreign Countries. New York: World Trade Academy Press. Data on more than 4,200 American corporations which control and operate over 16,500 foreign business enterprises. Indexed alphabetically and geographically.

Directory of Career Training and Development Programs. Santa Monica, CA: Ready Reference Press. A guide to career training and development opportunities available from business, government, and professional organizations. Includes management training programs, summer training programs, professional development programs, operations development programs, field sales training programs, and special development programs.

Directory of College Recruiting Personnel. Bethlehem, PA: College Placement Council. For almost 1,400 large employers, and 42 government agencies, provides name of organization, address, nature of business, number of employees, whether it recruits nationally or regionally, and the names, titles, and contact information for key college relations and recruiting personnel.

Directory of Corporate Affiliations. Skokie, IL: National Register Publishing Company, annually with supplements. Often called "Who Owns Whom," outlines corporate structure of major U.S. companies, their divisions, subsidiaries, and affiliates, both domestic and foreign.

Directory of Directories. James M. Ethridge, Editor. Detroit: Gale Research Company. Over 5,000 directories are described and indexed. Arranged in 15 major classifications and more than 2,100 subject headings. Includes state industrial directories and directories relating to business, education, government, science, public affairs.

Directory of National Unions and Employee Associations. Washington, D.C.: U.S. Department of Labor, Bureau of Labor Statistics. Lists names and addresses of national and international unions, state labor organizations, and professional and public employee associations. Includes their officers and key officials, publications, convention information, membership data, and number of locals.

Directory of Special Programs for Minority Group Members: Career Information Services, Employment Skills Banks, Financial Aid Sources. Willis L. Johnson, Editor. Garrett Park, MD: Garrett Park Press. Provides Black, Hispanic, Asian, and Native American candidates with a listing and description of special programs. Includes over 2,000 national and local organizations, 400 federally-funded programs, and hundreds sponsored by individual colleges and universities.

Dun & Bradstreet Reference Book of Corporate Managements. New

York: Dun & Bradstreet. Contains data regarding directors and selected officers of approximately 2,400 companies with annual sales of $20 million or more and/or 1,000 or more employees. Data include date of birth, education, and business positions presently and previously held.

Encyclopedia of Associations. Volume 1. National Organizations of the U.S. Detroit: Gale Research Company. For nonprofit American membership organizations of national scope, gives location, size, objectives, and other descriptors of thousands of trade associations, professional societies, labor unions, others. Particularly useful for securing information about scientific, social and, industrial fields where change is rapid. A key word index aids location of organizations associated with particular subjects.

Facts on File: World News Digest. Stephen Orlofsky, Managing Editor. New York: Facts on File, Inc., weekly. The News Digest is a summary of what is reported in more than 50 foreign and U.S. newspapers and magazines. It includes up-to-date information on subjects, people, organizations, countries, and U.S. companies.

F&S Index of Corporations and Industries. George Cratcha, Editor. Cleveland, OH: Predicasts, Inc., weekly. Covers company, product and industry information from over 750 financial publications, business-oriented newspapers, trade magazines, and special reports. Includes up-to-date information on corporate acquisitions and mergers, new products, technological developments, and socio-political factors. Also reports on trends in business and finance, corporate management and labor relations, and general economic factors.

Forbes Annual Report on American Industry. Forbes Magazine, annually. Profitability, growth, and market performance of the 1,035 largest U.S. public companies and the 31 major U.S. industrial groups, rated on the Forbes Yardsticks. Reports and projections for 22 industries, from Aerospace to Utilities.

Guide to American Directories. Coral Springs, FL: B. Klein Publications. Provides information on directories published by business and reference book publishers, magazines, trade associations, chambers of commerce, and by city, state, and federal government agencies. Entries are categorized under some 300 industrial, technical, mercantile, scientific, and professional headings from Accounting to Wire and Wire Products. Special attention is called to the section on Employment Services, containing an extensive listing of directories helpful to job seekers.

Guide to Corporations: A Social Perspective. Council on Economic

Priorities. Chicago: Swallow Press, 1974. Detailed profiles of 43 major U.S. corporations, arranged alphabetically within industries. Profiles include information on products marketed to the public, financial data, how cooperative the corporation is about disclosing relevant information, pollution control expenditures, military contracting, and equal opportunity for minority groups and women.

International Jobs: Where They Are, How to Get Them. Eric Kocher. Garrett Park, MD: Garrett Park Press. Guide to over 300 career opportunities in business, private agencies, government, and international organizations around the world. Includes section on job hunting strategies for overseas employment.

Job Prospector. Waltham, MA: Prospector Research Services, Inc., monthly. Reports new expansions by industry, commerce, and institutions to guide those interested in new job opportunities (within the New York, New Jersey, southern Connecticut area).

Million Dollar Directory and *Middle Market Directory.* New York: Dun & Bradstreet, annually. For each of approximately 39,000 U.S. companies with an indicated worth of $1 million or more, the Million Dollar Directory lists officers and directors, products or services, approximate sales, and number of employees. Includes indexes by geographic location and by industry. The Middle Market Directory, listing about 31,000 companies, covering companies with an indicated worth of from $500,000 to $999,999, provides similar data.

Moody's Industrial Manual. Two Volumes. New York: Moody's Investors Service, Inc., annually. For many thousands of companies, provides history, description of business and products, principal plants and properties, top management, and extensive financial data. Volume one includes a classification of companies by industries and products (Advertising to Zinc).

Note: The publisher also produces the following books providing similar data on potential employers other than industrial companies.

Moody's Municipal & Government Manual
Moody's Bank & Finance Manual
Moody's Public Utility Manual
Moody's Transportation Manual

The Multinational Marketing and Employment Directory. New York: World Trade Academy Press. For more than 7,500 American corporations operating in the U.S. and overseas, gives addresses, products or services, names of president and personnel director. Also has a guide for selling skills according to professions and occupations.

The New York Times Index. New York: The New York Times Company, twice a month and annually. Abstracts of news and editorial matter appearing in the Times, entered under headings arranged alphabetically. Each entry is followed by a reference to date, page, and column. Related headings are covered by cross-references or duplicate entries.

Occupational Outlook Handbook. Washington, D.C.: U.S. Department of Labor, Bureau of Labor Statistics, every other year. For 850 occupations in 35 major industries, provides information on what the work is like, job prospects for the next decade, personal qualifications, training and educational requirements, working conditions, earnings, chances for advancement, and contact sources for additional information. Supplemented by Occupational Outlook Quarterly, available from same source.

Readers' Guide to Periodical Literature. New York: H. W. Wilson, annually. Cumulative author/subject index to some 160 periodicals of general interest published in the U.S. Authors and subjects are arranged in one alphabet. Subdivisions of a subject are arranged alphabetically under the subject. Geographical subheads follow the other subdivisions in a separate alphabet. Source for current information on potential employers or possible career choices.

Standard & Poor's Industry Surveys. Two Volumes. New York: Standard & Poor's Corporation, annually. Analysis of 69 major domestic industries, divided into 34 segments (Aerospace to Utilities). Information includes analysis of outlook, national and world developments, marketing, financial and statistical data, individual companies.

Standard & Poor's Register of Corporations, Directors and Executives. Three Volumes. New York: Standard & Poor's Corporation, annually. Volume One is an alphabetical listing of over 36,000 U.S. and Canadian companies; provides officers, products or line of business, sales range, and number of employees. Volume Two is a list of executives and directors, with brief data about each. Volume Three includes an index of companies by location.

Standard Corporation Descriptions. Six Volumes. New York: Standard & Poor's Corporation, semi-monthly. Detailed, timely information on corporate background, operations, finances, key personnel changes, and important news concerning many thousands of companies, listed alphabetically.

Standard Directory of Advertisers. Skokie, IL: National Register Publishing Company, annually with monthly supplements. Often referred to as the "Advertiser Red Book," this is a guide to over

17,000 corporations which advertise. Listings include name, contact information, products or services, some key executives (primarily top and marketing management), and name of advertising agency. A trade name index provides name of advertiser when only product name is known.

Standard Periodical Directory. Howard Greenberg, Editor. New York: Oxbridge Communications. Directory of U.S. and Canadian periodicals, including magazines, trade journals, newsletters, government publications, house organs, directories, yearbooks, and so on. Entries are indexed under 230 subject categories from Accounting to Zoology. Each entry describes the publication available and includes contact information. Special attention is called to section 0600, Employment, where a large number of useful area-specific periodicals are listed.

Ulrich's International Periodicals Directory. New York: R. R. Bowker, annually. Some 62,000 periodicals of all kinds from all over the world in some 250 subject areas. Each entry provides title, frequency of publication, publisher name and address, country of publication, and Dewey Decimal Classification number. Entries arranged by subject, Advertising to Water Resources. Special attention is called to listings under "Occupations and Careers."

Who's Who in America. Two Volumes. Chicago: Marquis Who's Who, Inc. Biographical data on some 72,000 influential people. Each entry provides such information as name, position, vital statistics, education, family status, career and career-related activities, civic and political activities, writings, address.
Note: The publisher also produces the following books which include many entries not found in "Who's Who in America," and are equally useful: Who's Who in the Midwest; . . . in the East; . . . in the South and Southwest; . . . in the West; . . . of American Women; . . . in Government; . . . in Science; . . . in Finance and Industry; . . . in American Law; . . . in the World; . . . Biographical Record — School District Officials; Marquis Who's Who Publications/Index to All Books.

Work Related Abstracts. Detroit: Information Coordinators, Inc., monthly. Extracts from over 250 management, labor, government, professional, and university periodicals. Subjects include Careers, Career Development, Job Hunting, Job Satisfaction, Occupational Choice, Training Programs (business, government), Vocational Guidance, Vocational Interest, information on specific large companies and government departments.

Appendix C:
Innovative Resumes

Reproduced on pages following are resumes, sections of resumes, and resume attachments written by graduating seniors who demonstrated their ability to create innovative, highly effective resumes by going beyond the typical approaches normally employed.

If I Had Gone to NYU or Columbia, We'd Have Already Met.

But since I'm going to graduate school in the southwest, it's not that easy for us to get together. So let me take a few minutes to introduce myself.

My name is Bill Bergman and this August I'll graduate from SMU with a Masters of Business Administration.

As a career goal, I want to work on an account team of a large advertising agency.

Now for a 22-year old, attaining a goal like that isn't easy. It takes years of busting your brains in the library, gaining practical experience, and developing the discipline to work 25 hours a day.

Sure. Advertising is tough to break into. But if you've been trained like I have, meeting the competition head on is what makes the business so exciting.

Undergraduate Education

In May of 1974, I graduated from the University of Oklahoma with a bachelors degree in advertising through the school of journalism.

As a junior, I won the Leslie Rice Memorial Award in Advertising. And as a senior, I was elected into Kappa Tau Alpha, the national journalism scholarship society.

My activities as an undergraduate included three years on the campus newspaper where I served as wire editor, staff writer, and columnist.

I was president of the Stewart Harrell chapter of the Public Relations Student Society of America and managing editor of their national publication, the *Forum*.

As a member of the OU debate team, I participated in intercollegiate debate tournaments on such topics as national health care.

During my junior year, I was a resident advisor in a freshman dormitory of 60 screaming maniacs.

Finally, I was a pledge trainer of the Alpha Epsilon Pi social fraternity.

Work Experience

Presently, I'm doing an internship with Glenn, Bozell & Jacobs here in Dallas. Working with the account team in charge of packaged goods, I've done everything from writing client contact reports to aiding in development of marketing plans.

Last summer, I worked at Tempo Advertising in New Orleans, my hometown. There, I served as an assistant account executive working on several accounts including an amusement park and a local rootbeer bottler.

Late in the summer, I was employed by Crain Publications as a student assistant to their annual *Advertising Age* Creative Workshop in New York.

My first taste of the agency business came in the summer of 1972 when I was an office boy at Peter Mayer Advertising.

The next summer I returned to that agency, this time in the account services department doing marketing research for the agency's biggest client, Wembley Ties.

A Determined MBA

I've been working too hard and too long to let a couple of hundred miles get in my way.

More than anything, I want to go into the agency business. And I've got the motivation, maturity, and education to prove it.

If you'd like to meet me or have some references sent, write me at my school address:

5200 Belmont
Apt. 220
Dallas, Texas 75206
(214) 824-3983

or at my permanent home address:

2114 Jefferson Ave.
New Orleans, Louisiana 70115
(504) 891-6531

SOUTHERN METHODIST UNIVERSITY

Of special interest: 1. Outstanding resume from a person who makes it as clear as possible that he wants to be in advertising — he writes an ad selling himself. 2. A perfect followup to his undergraduate resume (see Figure 6.8). 3. His unique, highly professional approach attracts immediate attention and persuades the reader to see him.

Dear Mr. Rogers,

I will be in New York City between January 2 and 6, 1979, and would appreciate the chance to meet with you. I look forward to hearing from you. Thank you

J.A. Quittner

Judith Anne Quittner
2402 Clark Ave., Apt.2,
Raleigh, N.C. 27607
919-832-1456

Personal:

I will graduate in May, 1979, from North Carolina State University with a Bachelor of Arts in Visual Design, and a minor in Graphics and Communications. I was born in Pennsylvania on August 27, 1956, and lived there until 1974. Since then I have lived in North Carolina. I am single, in excellent health, 5'8", 135 pounds. I am interested in employment and relocating in May.

Some of my professional activities have been:

a poster for the multiple sclerosis Foundation;
logo for the "Save the Whales" campaign;
ad design for the "Technician", the NCSU student paper;
worked with Walt Obman, free-lance designer;
a flyer for Dave's Beetle Barn;
assisted in the conception and completion of two 5' x 8' wallhangings for the N.C. Museum of Art;
created and produced a 30 second TV spot on bicycle safety for the N.C. Department of Transportation;
and, held an internship with McKinney, Silver and Rocket Advertising.

Some of my accomplishments are:

aphganistan rug weaving, learned at the University of Pennsylvania;
dean's list;
water-safety-instructor's license;
photography;
water and snow skiing;
macrame and sewing;
hair cutting;
jewelry retail;
waitressing;
health food and wine retail;
volunteer at Easter Seals Day Camp;
PMT's, typositors, compugraphic type setting, enlargers, x-acto knives, and magic marker operations.

My employment interests are:

book, pamphlet and brochure design;
typography, photography, and illustration;
package design;
sign and symbol creation;
advertising design;
exhibit and display design.

Of special interest: 1. This resume's graphics readily stand out among most others. 2. Employs "human contact" by being personalized with salutation line and her signature. 3. Manifests her interest in art and visual design. Conveys the professionalism she hopes will earn her an interview. 4. Resume is effective without citing details of employment experience. 5. This was a "self-mailer"—folded in thirds and stapled closed, with the stamp and address on one-third of the back.

RICKI DILLMAN

6 PEARL DRIVE

ROCKLAND, CALIFORNIA 90017

(213) 555-3617*

I SEEK:	An entry level position in the Media department of an advertising agency.
I'M DRIVEN:	I am highly motivated by new learning experiences. I am comfortable working with numbers and am enthused about the prospect of dealing with Media functions. My self-discipline, creativity and assertiveness enable me to communicate readily and effectively.
I'M EDUCATED:	Ohio University, B.A., Communications, May, 1977.
I'VE WORKED:	Starting with my early teenage years, I've pursued a wide variety of part-time and summer positions. I've sold real estate by phone, vacuum cleaners door-to-door, clothing in a high quality boutique, and hamburgers in a fast-food chain. I've clerked, typed, filed and done countless office chores. I've learned that you have to pay your dues in the business world, and I'm ready to start at the bottom so that I can show I have what it takes for a shot at the top.
I'M VITAL:	My interests include reading, travel, camping, writing, music, photography.
I AM:	Female, single, age 21, in excellent health, anxious to get started.

*Messages may be left with Anne Dillman at (213) 974-6030.

Of special interest: 1. Getting away from traditional section headings such as "Objective," "Education," and "Experience," can make for an out-of-the-ordinary resume. 2. Note how effectively she has related previous experience to her goal, without beclouding the reader's perusal with a recitation of summer and part-time jobs. 3. Her approach permitted her to project personal attributes in three sections ("I'm Driven," "I've Worked," "I Am"). 4. By offering a number where messages could be left, she facilitated employer contact.

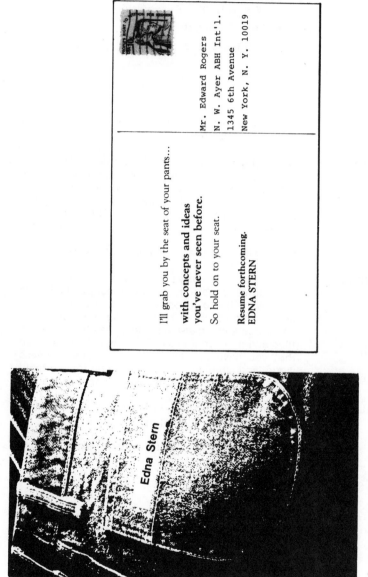

I'll grab you by the seat of your pants...

**with concepts and ideas
you've never seen before.**

So hold on to your seat.

**Resume forthcoming.
EDNA STERN**

Mr. Edward Rogers
N. W. Ayer ABH Int'l.
1345 6th Avenue
New York, N. Y. 10019

Edna Stern

(On this and the next two pages) Of special interest: 1. Postcard was mailed three to four days before the resume. 2. This attractive resume was printed on 11" x 17" paper, folded to 8½" x 11", with resume on one side and space for personalized cover letter on the other. 3. Headings, trim lines, and typed letter were in blue; resume copy in gray — very handsome to look at.

August 15, 1980

Mr. Edward J. Rogers
Vice President, Director of Personnel
N. W. Ayer ABH International
1345 Avenue of the Americas
New York, N.Y. 10019

Dear Mr. Rogers,

When a person puts her name on a product
she is telling others that she believes
in it; that the product represents quality,
fine craftsmanship. My ideas are my product. They are excitingly different and
totally appropriate for the needs of my
clients.

I am proud of my work and I would like the
opportunity to share it with you. I know
I can be a creative contribution to N. W.
Ayer ABH International. With the name
Edna Stern behind you, success is, as they
say, "in the pocket."

Hoping to hear from you soon,

Edna Stern

**Career Objective: Advertising
Art Director position using my
Graphic Design, business, and
leadership abilities.**

Edna Dianne Stern

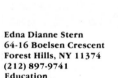

Edna Dianne Stern
64-16 Boelsen Crescent
Forest Hills, NY 11374
(212) 897-9741

Education

Carnegie-Mellon University
B.F.A. Graphic Design with a
minor degree in business.
QPA 3.6

Technical Experience
Typography: Handset Type
Photocomposition:
  Compugraphic, Varityper
Photography: Color, Black and
  White
Printing Production Methods
Advanced Color Workshop
Marketing One and Two
Organizational Behavior One and
  Two
Elements of Industrial
  Administration
Product Marketing Analysis

Forest Hills High School
Honor graduate, Artwork
exhibited in "Outstanding Artists
in New York City School
Exhibition."
Member of Human Resource
Administration
"Executive High School
Internship Program."
Recipient of BACA Honors
Painting Scholarship.

Positions Held

University Graphics
A student-controlled advertising
agency. Executive Director.
Promoted from Art Director by
the University Committee.
1977-1980

The Graphic Suite
Coordinator of client presentations. Design consultant.
1979-1980

Center for Juvenile Justice
Designer for brochure series on
juvenile justice in America. 1980

Mellon Institute
Creative Director for Egypt/Israel
communications booklet.
1979-1980

Berner International
Art Director responsible for all
aspects of promotional material.
1979-1980

CMU Public Relations
Assisted in the recruitment for
publicity. 1979-1980

Satelite Air Services
Art Director for World Trade
Center promotional. Spring 1979

Unlimited Wallpaper Inc.
Ongoing freelance design work.
Generation of wallpaper patterns,
exhibition design and advertising
design. 1978-1980

**Pajama Corporation of
America**
Production designer. Summer
1977

Shima/Passberger Advertising
Internship. Learning all aspects of
advertising. 1976-1977

**Pappert, Koening and Lois
  Advertising**
Internship. 1976

Honors:

Senior Degree Show
Public presentation of juried
senior project.

Women In Communications
Vice-president and co-founder of
Carnegie-Mellon organization.

Forbes Street Gallery
Exhibited in three person show.

Outside Activities:

Tri-Delta sorority member.
Chairman of Design Issues
Lecture Series.

Interests:

Travel, tennis, and painting.

**References and portfolio
furnished upon request.**

```
UNDERSTANDING
PEOPLE         *I communicate well with people.  As a Resident Assistant, I
                supervised 30 undergraduates, often helping them cope with
                academic, social and emotional difficulties and was on call 24
                hours a day, seven days a week.
               *As a tennis professional at The Concord Hotel, Kiamesha Lake,
                N.Y. and The Broome Racquet Club, Binghamton, N.Y., I instructed
                individuals of varying ages, personalities and talents which has
                strengthened my ability to effectively communicate with many
                different types of people.
               *As the Community Affairs Chairman of the Tau Alpha Upsilon
                fraternity, I conceived and organized a Big Brother program for
                less fortunate Binghamton area boys which met with success and
                praise from the civic and campus communities.
               *As a member of the College Judicial Board, I presided over
                hearings concerning student grievances and infractions of
                University regulations.
```

Of special interest: 1. Unusual section to find on a resume, yet one of great interest to most employers. 2. Note how he logically explains how various school activities and work experience contributed to his understanding of others (section of resume by Neal J. Roher).

RESUME

Miriam Suchoff
2220 Country Club Drive
Woodridge, Illinois 60515
Tel:(312)960-2642

> "If we could have a Renaissance Woman--and why not?--
> Miriam Suchoff would be she. This remarkable person
> has become a communications generalist with superior
> developed skills, acquired through natural ability,
> education and experience. Especially noteworthy are
> her demonstrated and documented-leadership skills.
> I am most familiar with her accomplishments as editor-
> in-chief of Boston University's all-university yearbook.
> Because of special circumstances, Miriam assumed leader-
> ship amid an almost impossible collection of problems
> and barriers till the book's completion. That she did
> so cheerfully with enormous energy, vigor and dedication
> is completely in character; that she did so successfully
> is evidence of her ability to solve problems most persons
> would shy away from."
>
> Excerpt from letter of recommendation
> by Norman Bryden, University teacher,
> consultant,critic and author.

QUALIFICATIONS

INITIATIVE AND MOTIVATION
    While matriculating, founded and organized entire operation for
    the College Advertising Service, a poster distribution service
    for businesses catering to college market. Signed ten accounts
    in the first six weeks (client list available upon request).
    Handled design, layout and printing of posters for my accounts.
    Also responsible for bookkeeping and bill collecting.

LEADERSHIP SKILLS
    Editor-in-chief of the Boston University yearbook Hub '76.
    Supervised a staff of 25 volunteers; coordinated and guided copy,
    photo and layout deadlines to meet production deadlines. Edited
    all copy, approved all final layouts and organized ladder diagram
    for the publication. Acted as liaison for staff and Boston Uni-
    versity administration, Previous position on this yearbook staff,
    Business Manager; designed media plan, organized procedure for
    soliciting advertisers, sold ads for the yearbook, devised a sales
    campaign to overcome university-wide apathy. Success of campaign
    evident by record yearbook sales.

COMMUNICATION SKILLS
    As free lancer, designed logo and camera-ready ads for three local
    restaurants; executed camera-ready trade publication ad for whole-
    sale veal business. As a consultant, obtained client through the
    College Advertising Service; designed logo, designed/edited booklet,
    designed/edited newsletter. Ability to communicate verbally enhanced
    through experience as saleswoman for men's clothing store and Account
    Executive for College Advertising Service.

Of special interest: 1. Example of unusual placement and effective use of an extremely
strong recommendation. 2. This is page one of her two-page functional resume.

What is _not_ in this resume'

This is the fourth rewrite of my resume' but try as I might, important things are not in it.

Things like a skinny little kid growing up in a dusty Oklahoma town called Nicoma Park learning about work and what Grandmother Clark called "bein' true to yourself." Or at 13 learning "commerce" in Grandfather Morrison's hardware store or later getting up before dawn for $1 an hour and spending it all on the second fastest '57 Chevy in town. Then there was college with more freshmen enrolled than there were people in all of Nicoma Park. And after I had that down, a dirty war in a speck of jungle called Viet Nam. Then a lady named Vicki who brought me out of my personal piece of that jungle.

Last chapter: a full-time job as one of "them": a university administrator and finishing the Masters.

Then again, maybe these aren't things that belong in a resume' but they're important to me and somehow I hope they are to you.

Of special interest: 1. Projects a sincere, involved, mature writer, deserving of an interview. Good example of "human contact." 2. This attachment was printed on the back of the resume, filling one panel when the resume was folded in thirds for envelope insertion.

Lori Silverstein
P.R. Inc.
1 Madonia Court
Plandome Manor, New York 11030
(516) 365-8127

<u>For Immediate Release</u>

<u>SILVERSTEIN'S SUGAR-PLUM READY FOR THE BIG APPLE</u>

David Silverstein, a prominent Minneapolis builder, gratefully announces that he has paid his last tuition bill for his daughter, Lori. "She's ready to get a job," stated Silverstein, "and I'm ready to shift her onto someone else's payroll!"

"A chip off the old block," Silverstein went on. "I could use her back in Minneapolis, but she prefers The Big Apple. While at Hofstra University, Lori developed public relations campaigns, news and feature press releases, wrote creative advertising copy and, in my judgment, gained a good business sense."

"Eight years of part-time job experience in merchandising and sales, many scholastic honors (see enclosed resume)..." David Silverstein said that he could go on and on, but to quote an old Chinese proverb--- "An interview is worth a thousand words."

Of special interest: 1. Demonstrates her interest in public relations by using a "press release" rather than a cover letter. 2. Her clever writing style involves the reader — sure to earn her better-than-average response from potential employers.

HIRE THIS WOMAN

You're a growth firm. Your best resource is your managers. You want only the best.

Consider Lezli White

She likes challenge. And her background proves not only her drive and determination, it proves her ability.

She was among the first women to graduate from the ivy covered halls of Williams College. She has a Master of Science in journalism from America's top school, home of the Pulitzer prize-Columbia. She has a Masters in Business Administration from Columbia's Graduate School of Business. Not a small accomplishment for the first college graduate in a family.

Choose Lezli White

It takes more than degrees you say. She has worked in many phases of television. She is a published writer and photographer. She produces her own weekly radio show. She creates advertising and promotion for a jazz poetry group.

So she knows why when where and what to communicate— and how to do it effectively.

She's a hard worker, a quick learner and a self starter.

These days this kind of intelligence, effectiveness, and competence is always needed.

Do yourself a service. Hire Lezli White

Plan for the long range. Full service person for the full service company.

Of special interest: 1. Accompanied a "traditional" resume. Demonstrates that MBA's, who typically approach resume writing in a highly conservative manner, can successfully take an innovative approach to job-seeking. 2. Synopsizes her credentials in a most appealing way.

Zero to sixty in 4 years.

In a high-performance business like advertising, it takes more than just a sheepskin and good intentions to get ahead.

I'm Tim Kane.

Over the past four years, I've worked on over 60 different accounts. Writing. Designing. Getting experience in everything from broadcast to billboards.

"Impressive track record," you say. "But what's under the hood?"

I'll be getting my degree from Michigan State this June. A B.A. in advertising — summa cum laude, yet. I'm a National Merit Scholar, too.

Economy? Manageability?

I run on that special blend of high-octane enthusiasm and fresh-out-of-college confidence. Add my experience — and some of your agency's polish — and we'll really burn rubber.

Give my portfolio a test run. And let the others eat our dust.

KANE*

Of special interest: 1. This attachment clearly and creatively conveys the writer's field of interest. It is sure to be read. 2. His copy demonstrates his awareness of the "lingo" used by those in his desired occupation.

Appendix D:
Fifty Questions
Prospective Employers Ask

1. What are your long range and short range goals and objectives, when and why did you establish these goals, and how are you preparing yourself to achieve them?
2. What specific goals, other than those related to your occupation, have you established for yourself for the next 10 years?
3. What do you see yourself doing five years from now?
4. What do you *really* want to do in life?
5. What are your long range career objectives?
6. How do you plan to achieve your career goals?
7. What are the most important rewards you expect in your business career?
8. What do you expect to be earning in five years?
9. Why did you choose the career for which you are preparing?
10. Which is more important to you, the money or the type of job?
11. What do you consider to be your greatest strengths and weaknesses?
12. How would you describe yourself?
13. How do you think a friend or professor who knows you well would describe you?
14. What motivates you to put forth your greatest effort?
15. How has your college experience prepared you for a business career?
16. Why should I hire you?
17. What qualifications do you have that make you think that you will be successful in business?
18. How do you determine or evaluate success?
19. What do you think it takes to be successful in a company like ours?
20. In what ways do you think you can make a contribution to our company?
21. What qualities should a successful manager possess?
22. Describe the relationship that should exist between a supervisor and those reporting to him or her.
23. What two or three accomplishments have given you the most satisfaction? Why?
24. Describe your most rewarding college experience.
25. If you were hiring a graduate for this position, what qualities would you look for?

26. Why did you select your college or university?
27. What led you to choose your field of major study?
28. What college subjects did you like best? Why?
29. What college subjects did you like least? Why?
30. If you could do so, how would you plan your academic study differently? Why?
31. What changes would you make in your college or university? Why?
32. Do you have plans for continued study? An advanced degree?
33. Do you think that your grades are a good indication of your academic achievement?
34. What have you learned from participation in extra-curricular activities?
35. In what kind of a work environment are you most comfortable?
36. How do you work under pressure?
37. In what part-time or summer jobs have you been most interested? Why?
38. How would you describe the ideal job for you following graduation?
39. Why did you decide to seek a position with this company?
40. What do you know about our company?
41. What two or three things are most important to you in your job?
42. Are you seeking employment in a company of a certain size? Why?
43. What criteria are you using to evaluate the company for which you hope to work?
44. Do you have a geographical preference? Why?
45. Will you relocate? Does relocation bother you?
46. Are you willing to travel?
47. Are you willing to spend at least six months as a trainee?
48. Why do you think you might like to live in the community in which our company is located?
49. What major problem have you encountered and how did you deal with it?
50. What have you learned from your mistakes?

*Source: The Endicott Report, 1975. Published and copyrighted by the Placement Center, Northwestern University, Evanston, Illinois.

Appendix E:
Factor Analysis
of Job Offer Alternatives *

For those who take the time, a factor analysis of any job offer will prove advantageous. It allows you to look at the problem incrementally, to make a large decision through a series of smaller ones which reduce confusion. This procedure is divided into two stages: (1) *design*, the initial preparation of the DAC (Decision/Analysis Chart), which helps you evaluate and rate crucial job considerations in terms of your needs and requirements; and (2) *application*, the use of the DAC in the analysis of a specific employment situation.

The following list is a sampling of items related to employee benefits, compensations, and working conditions which a job hunter might investigate before accepting a particular position. If you are considering an offer, make a personal list of the elements that are most important to you and find out how well the organization in question compares in these areas with others in the field. The items presented here are not inclusive; they are only examples for reference — they may not relate to your particular situation or reflect your interests. You must decide here what your personal priorities are. The time to make a decision in terms of yourself is *before* a job is accepted. Which conditions of employment are most important to you, the applicant?

1. Initial salary and raise schedule
2. Sick leave payment
3. Separation allowance (severance pay)
4. Old-age, survivors', disability, and health insurance
5. Travel and per diem compensation
6. Worker's compensation
7. Bonuses, commissions, and other compensations
8. Credit union
9. Union affiliation
10. Service awards

*Source: "How to See if a Job Is Right" by Ross Figgins. Reprinted with permission of PERSONNEL JOURNAL, Costa Mesa, CA, copyright December 1978; all rights reserved.

11. Chances for advancement
12. Company-paid education programs
13. Paid holidays
14. Unemployment compensation
15. Management incentives
16. Special clothing allowances
17. Necessity to relocate
18. Pension plans
19. Special company training programs
20. Paid vacations
21. Reimbursement for moving
22. Potential for advancement within company
23. Job safety record
24. Travel requirements
25. Purchasing discounts for employees
26. Suggestion bonuses
27. Size of organization
28. Major health plans
29. Tax-sheltered annuities
30. Number of supervisors
31. Overtime requirements and pay
32. Degree of privacy
33. Profit-sharing programs
34. Employee thrift plans
35. Degree of independence
36. Retirement plan
37. Job security
38. Geographic location
39. Amount of travel required
40. Patent or publication rights

The DAC begins with the identification and ranking of those factors
that you deem most important in a job — six to ten from the preceding list should be sufficient for analysis. In the example below,
the applicant is a young business graduate applying for sales positions
with a number of plastics companies. She feels that the following ten
items are paramount considerations for her in any position she
accepts:

1. Salary and raise schedule
2. Sick leave payment

3. Travel and per diem compensation
4. Bonuses, commissions, and other compensations
5. Chances for advancement
6. Company-paid education programs
7. Paid holidays
8. Reimbursement for moving
9. Paid vacations
10. Major health plans

The next step is to rank these in terms of personal priority. The applicant asks, "How strongly will each of these factors affect my final decision to work for a company?" Dividing them into three categories helps clarify the decision at this stage:

STRONG
☐ Salary
☐ Travel
☐ Education programs
MODERATE
☐ Bonuses, commissions
☐ Chances for advancement
☐ Sick leave payment
☐ Paid vacations
WEAK
☐ Major health plans
☐ Reimbursement for moving
☐ Paid holidays

Once an applicant has decided that certain factors in a potential position are more important than others, it is time to indicate how *much* more important they are when compared to one another. This weighting is done by assigning a numerical value to each item on the list; a scale from 1 to 10 works well. Notice that this is a subjective process; therefore, all numbers in the scale need not be used, and some factors may have virtually equal value to the individual.

STRONG
☐ Salary   8
☐ Travel   6
☐ Education program   7

MODERATE

☐	Bonuses, commissions	5
☐	Chances for advancement	4
☐	Sick leave payment	4
☐	Paid vacations	5

WEAK

☐	Major health plans	2
☐	Reimbursement for moving	1
☐	Paid holidays	3

The final step of this stage of employment analysis is simply to re-order the factors, in terms of their relative importance, and enter them on a Decision/Analysis Chart.

The second part of the factor analysis requires the applicant to apply the DAC scale to the specific company under consideration and evaluate how well it meets the criteria. In Table E.1, the Tridee Plastics Corporation is rated on each of the ten factors, using a five-point scale of poor (1) to superior (5). Each item is analyzed, a total score is calculated by multiplying the item's weight by the rating assigned to it, and the reason for the score is noted. This last step, writing out your reasoning, should not be ignored; it will increase objectivity and thereby the validity of the analysis.

When the chart is completed, the applicant can see how well one company, Tridee Plastics, compares to her employment require-ments. Or if there happen to be two or more positions under consid-eration she will fill out an additional DAC, total the number of points awarded each, and use the resulting total index ratings to compare them and discover where they differ. She could also use this approach when considering leaving a current position, for it will objectively quantify her alternatives.

Finally, in the sometimes delicate area of negotiating, an appli-cant can use information discovered in a factor analysis to pinpoint items for mediation. The earlier strong-moderate-weak ranking can instantly be transformed into a negotiation scale:

Strong	=	*Hard* Considerations
Moderate	=	*Firm* Considerations
Weak	=	*Soft* Considerations

"Hard" items are those which will affect an applicant's decision to work for a company. Characteristically, they have a bottom line, beyond which an offer is unacceptable. Efforts in negotiation should

Table E.1 Decision/Analysis Chart:*   Tridee Plastics

Factor	Weight	Poor (1)	Fair (2)	Good (3)	Excellent (4)	Superior (5)	Total	Reason for Rating
Salary	8			3			24	Straight salary. No commissions. Annual bonus (3%). All raises on merit only.
Education	7					5	35	Encouraged. Paid in full by the company through M.B.A. Salary-linked increments.
Travel	6				4		24	Mileage and per diem paid. No expense accounts.
Bonuses	5		2				10	No incentive bonuses or commissions. Annual 3% paid to all sales representatives.
Vacations	5				4		20	Two weeks paid annually — on a staggered basis. Company to give bonus for work.

Table E.1 (continued)

Factor	Weight	Poor (1)	Fair (2)	Good (3)	Excellent (4)	Superior (5)	Total	Reason for Rating
Sick leave	4			3			12	One day paid per month. No reimbursement plan for unused sick leave.
Holidays	3			3			9	Seven per year – paid.
Advancement	4					5	20	Policy of promotion from within. Most managers over 50 now.
Health plans	2	1					2	No company health plan.
Relocation	1	1					1	No reimbursement for new employees. Would have to move (400 miles).

TOTAL INDEX RATING: <u>157</u>

*From *Techniques of Job Search* by Ross Figgins. New York: Harper and Row, 1976. Copyright 1976 by Ross Figgins. Used with permission.

then be directed primarily at improving them. "Firm" refers to those factors that are important considerations to the applicant. They immediately follow "hard" factors, yet they may or may not affect your final decision drastically, depending of course on how well the former are mediated. Generally you should strive to improve the "firm" items whenever feasible. At the bottom of the mediation scale are the "soft" factors, those which are virtually unessential in terms of the preceding. Probably they will not seriously alter an employment decision, but can be considered valuable extras if included in the final terms.

To identify and rank employment options gives an applicant a clearer understanding of an often confusing situation and introduces the potential for assertive control in negotiations — which are, as likely as not, a series of small bargains. For example, since Tridee Plastics does not offer its employees a company-sponsored health program, "soft" on this applicant's scale, she may request one of her "hard" items, a higher starting salary, in order to offset the cost of joining a private program. Or because of graduation she may be moving soon anyway, and as Tridee does not pay for employee relocation, this gives her another trade item.

The use of factor analysis should not, however, limit one to consider and mediate only those items selected in the first stage; they represent one's personal criteria. If an employer offers other benefits, these naturally should be incorporated into the final decision.

One final word about decision making in employment situations — don't panic. Consider all options before making a final decision. Do not allow yourself to be pressured into a premature commitment. You should sincerely believe that the job you finally accept is the best available, and this belief should be supported by adequate objective information and analysis. Compare factors. Satisfy yourself that you have found what you want — a good employer and not just a job.

Index